FAITHFUL
AND
DEVOTED

FAITHFUL
AND
DEVOTED

CONFESSIONS OF A MUSIC ADDICT

JENNA ROSE ROBBINS

Printed in the United States of America

Library of Congress Control Number: 2017935109

ISBN Paperback: 978-0-9981760-6-2
ISBN eBook: 978-0-9981760-4-8

Design and illustrations: Lluvia Arras, www.lluviaarras.com
Interior Design: Ghislain Viau

In memory of Uncle Joe

ACKNOWLEDGEMENTS

So many of my friends have supported this work over the years, many of who believed in it more strongly than I did. It was at their urging that I turned a story often told at dinner parties into a full-fledged book, so you have them to either blame or thank.

In my first year of graduate school, my thesis advisor, Madelyn Cain, encouraged me to make my twelve-page essay the basis of my thesis. To this day, she continues to be one of the greatest supporters of my writing. Fellow music aficionado Shannon McClatchey continued to prod me when my creative juices were running on empty, while Marilyn Oliveira and Alysia Gray Painter provided their ample editorial experience to help me see the many holes that Swiss-cheesed my first draft. When it came time to design the book cover, there was only one person I ever considered: Lluvia Arras, whose artistic talents are rivaled only by her mutual love for the boys from Basildon, so I knew she would get the balance of fanaticism and aesthetics just right. And, of course, I probably would not have been the music lover I am today had it not been for my eldest sister, Janys, who is not shy of admitting that she hates to read and so will probably never know the extent of her inspiration.

PREFACE

When I decided to be a writer at the ripe old age of four, I never expected that the first book to bear my name on the cover would be a memoir. The spiral notebooks I filled with stories during my childhood could have filled a shopping cart, and not one of them was rooted in reality. Talking ferrets, shipwrecked teenagers, Victorian-esque ghosts, and even some Tolkien-inspired elves lived and breathed within those pages, and I'd always assumed one of these tales would be the first to escape the locked hope chest in the attic for a comparatively sunny bookstore shelf. I never would have predicted I'd be telling my tale before theirs.

But then, somewhere around 2005, while I was enrolled in a graduate writing program, I was tasked with writing a short memoir. After I read my paper in class, there was a flurry of questions from fellow classmates who either couldn't quite believe the level of my obsession or who got it and thanked me for putting their own feelings into words. It was the greatest literary acclaim I'd received since my second-grade opus *Fred the Frisky Ferret*.

A week later, I found myself in the office of the program director, who informed me he'd nominated my essay for an award. Soon after, my academic adviser had swayed me into making the story my thesis, even though the very reason I'd decided to attend graduate school was to complete a separate, non-memoir project that had been brewing in my craw and which I'd hoped would lead to a life of globe-hopping.

I also realized I'd already spent years telling and retelling the personal melodrama of that one week in Spain, so I might as well put it to paper and never have to tell it again. I also wanted others who'd been in my position to know they weren't alone—unlike how I'd felt at the end of that week. Despite being smack in the middle of a crowd of thousands, I'd never felt such utter despairing loneliness. And I'd had only myself to blame.

More than twenty years later, as I read my diary from that week, I hardly recognize the person who wrote it. But then a passage will reach out from the pages and resurrect that old tingle in my gut that makes me want to rush back out and do it all over again, consequences be damned.

My companion on this journey doesn't feel quite the same way. She and I still talk occasionally, when our time zones allow and when she deigns to open my email. When I told her last year that I was almost done with the book, there was silence on the other end of the internet. For a moment I thought the line had gone dead, but then I heard a hesitant "okay." She went on to say that she had no right to tell me not to publish my book and that she deserved having all her misdeeds recorded forever in ink and pixels. She verbally flogged herself for a good twenty minutes before I got a word in, at which point I told her I didn't hold any grudges and that my teenage self had been just as culpable as hers.

In the end, she asked only one favor of me: not to use her real name. I agreed, and she chose Marta. I chose "Paredes" as a fictional last name. Most everything else about her character is true, as I remember it, with the majority of the memories coming straight from my diary. I even read her the portion where she tricked me, a vegetarian, into eating pork rinds, which resulted in another vocal round of self-flagellation, despite her not remembering the incident. When I offered to send her a copy of the book so she could ask for edits, she declined. As far as I know, she still hasn't read it and has no intention of ever doing so. If she did, she'd probably make herself bear the burden of her church's *paso* on her own.

Many of my friends refer to this as my "Depeche Mode book," but I wrote this with the hopes that the reader could imagine any band or artist as the object of my obsession and still enjoy the ride as they learned what makes a music fanatic tick. The actual events are not so epic that I needed to share them. Rather, it's the absolute power that my obsession had over me that many people just can't fathom—until I've described the feelings that coursed through my body like raging teenage hormones. When I explain how the emotions gnawed at me, how they made me do things I knew were wrong, how they never ceased wanting more, more, *more*—then listeners seem to understand. I wrote this book for those readers, the ones who can't comprehend how an otherwise normal, responsible person could allow herself to be consumed by something so trivial as a mass-market music group—and for those who comprehend it all too well.

— Jenna Rose Robbins

PROLOGUE

ear Andy, Dave, Martin, and Alan,
At present we are in a hotel in Madrid preparing to leave for Barcelona. We saw your concert last night and in Pontevedra (Dave—we were in the front row making hand gestures during "Fly on the Windscreen" and "Behind the Wheel"—you sang to us) and then met you backstage (missed your chance, Dave) and went on to the clubs. We've both gone to extensive lengths to see your concerts. I came from the United States and Marta lied to her parents about where she was in order to be here. Together we've had a ton of adventures (some good, others not so good) and we only met each other face to face six days ago. We're writing this letter to thank you for how much you've influenced our lives. It's hard to imagine where we'd be had we never heard your music. One thing's for certain: we wouldn't be in this hotel.

We have so much to thank you for: inspiration, incredible music, even our friendship, mine and Marta's. We became friends through

1

Bong and had been writing to each other for little over a year when Marta invited me to Spain to meet her and to see your concerts. We can't tell you how it made us feel when we met you and saw that you were just as great—even better—in person than we had imagined. I know at least for me, the thrill of meeting the people behind my inspiration for most everything I do, whether it's writing, photography or what have you, is something I will carry with me for the rest of my life and well worth all the trouble we've been through (and are still in). As of today, we have traveled over 47 hours (mostly on cold, cramped, uncomfortable trains standing up), lost 10,000 pesetas in Pontevedra, been attacked by drunken men on city streets, hauled a ten-ton suitcase through Madrid, told our parents we would be someplace other than where we were ("Yeah, Mom, we'll be at her house in León all the time." "Sí, Mama, I'm not going to see Depeche Mode. I'm going to my friend's house for a few days."), been caught lying by our parents, had people tell us we had to sleep with them to get backstage passes that already had our names on them (we found others), and fried ourselves in the sun waiting on line. We're having the time of our lives. (Book and movie to follow.) Our only regret is that after Barcelona, we can't see the rest of your tour.

Once again, 101 thanks. See you in Barcelona.

> Faithful and Devoted,
> Jenna Robbins &
> Marta Paredes

I t wasn't until I'd gone through airport customs that I even considered I'd made a mistake. At the luggage carousel, the doors opened every few moments to expose excited friends and family members bobbing their heads in the hopes of glimpsing loved ones. I didn't bother looking. I didn't know who I was looking for. The only thing I had to go on was a description: "long black hair and green eyes." I was in Madrid. Practically everyone around me fit that description.

I moved my luggage to a central area where I could be more easily spotted. Five, ten minutes passed. Must be rush-hour traffic, I thought, then realized it was a Saturday. No worries. A half hour later, sketchy Spanish men began to offer me rides—or a drink, I wasn't sure which. I had only a year and a half of Spanish on my college transcript, so they could have been reciting the recipe for flan and I wouldn't have known the difference. But I was from New York. At JFK, men—especially strange ones—offering rides was the norm. *No problemo.*

After forty-five minutes, uneasiness set in. Swarms of strangers had passed me without a second glance—they obviously weren't searching for a redheaded, 19-year-old *americana*. I fiddled with the tag on my hard-shelled suitcase, currently doubling as a seat in the crowded airport, and faced the facts: Marta wasn't coming. I remembered that my passport satchel contained a youth hostel card and glanced around for a telephone. The idea quickly vanished when I realized that making reservations would require speaking Spanish. It was my first time on foreign soil (Canada didn't count) and I was stranded without any clue of where to go or what to do next. But my greatest fear wasn't the thought of being in a foreign country by myself for the next several weeks. What I dreaded most was admitting to my mother that she had been right. The very thought made me want to hurl my in-flight meal.

From the moment I'd introduced the idea, my mother had fought it. "Spain? Why do you need to go to Spain? You're already going to France." She hadn't even looked up from bottle-feeding the orphaned raccoon she'd brought home from the vet's office where she worked. "Six weeks in France is quite enough." This last sentence was meant to settle the affair, just as similar statements had done in countless other mother-daughter debates over the years. But as far as I was concerned, the matter was far from settled.

I knew what I wanted, and Marta's most recent letter to me promised that my wildest dreams would come true—if only I would come, come to Spain. Her painstakingly perfect handwriting beckoned like a travel poster of a bygone era, luring me to the mysteries of the Iberian Peninsula. I'd been writing to Marta for only a year, much less time than I'd been writing to any of my other two dozen or so pen pals, but from the five or six letters we'd exchanged, I already felt a deep kinship, an understanding that went far beyond the typical angst teenagers share. Despite our different nationalities, we spoke the same covert language, so much so that I knew that my mother, were she ever to read our letters, would think we communicated in some sort of new-wave transatlantic slang that I'd learned from listening to CDs backwards.

My mother was used to being on the outside of my conversations. The summer before I left for college, my family hosted a French exchange student. Marion and I became fast friends, switching between our two languages depending on our mood and desired level of privacy. My mother would try to pick out a word here and there—"Cat! I know you were talking about a cat!"—but she could only manage a few French words, one of which was not Marion's name. "*Mary-on*," she would drone like some Southern hick on methadone, and I would roll my eyes. When I told her to pronounce it normally, "like an American," my mother still insisted on mangling our guest's name, infusing it with an accent that made my teenage-self cringe in embarrassment. "I'm saying it just the way you say it," she insisted.

In a roundabout way, it was because of Marion that I was in Spain. As part of the exchange program, I was to visit her the summer after her stay in the States. (Unbeknownst to both my parents, I had ticked the option of "reciprocal exchange" rather than "monetary compensation" on the host-family application.) Had I not already been planning a trip to France, I would never have considered hitting up my parents for two extra weeks in Spain.

I didn't *need* to go to Spain, I answered my mother, who was now picking a flea from the raccoon's groin. But I was already hopping the Pond, I reasoned, so why not make the most of the airfare? I didn't share my real reason for wanting to visit a second foreign country, knowing that it would only incite annoyance from the person who least understood my infatuation. My mother ignored my question and concentrated her efforts on dabbing the squirming raccoon, who had spit up evaporated milk on the front of her shirt.

Marta's letter of promises burned in my hand, urging me to press harder. I aimed for my mother's Achilles' heel. "It'll be a lot less expensive if I do both countries in one long trip, rather than crossing the ocean twice."

My mother shoved the bottle back in the raccoon's mouth. Finally, as the critter once again took to sucking, she sank into the chair, heaving the sigh of resignation I'd hoped for. Her back still to me, she said, "Ask your father. See what he says."

If there'd been such a thing as black pompoms, I would have been shaking them and doing cartwheels like the cheerleaders I so despised. I'd won the battle. There was no way my father would turn down an opportunity to expand my cultural and linguistic knowledge. I rushed to my candy-apple-red Firebird and sped across town to ask him. His grin nearly split his face in two and, moments later, he was calling over his colleagues to share in the celebration. "My daughter's going to Spain and France!" he announced to all who'd listen. And there were many. "She's going to practice her Spanish *and* French! She speaks two foreign languages, you know." In that respect, he was stretching the truth as much as his smile was splitting his face.

Although my father had agreed and my mother had gone along with his decision, in the weeks leading up to my departure, she prodded me with off-putting remarks. "Why Spain? You've never shown any interest in going there." My Spanish grades from the last two years must have somehow eluded her. I reminded her that in addition to having taken Spanish classes, I'd cared enough to seek out a pen pal in said country. But no matter what my response, she persisted, hoping to find a weakness. Her needling was endless, and soon she was voicing misgivings about the one area where I had little knowledge: Marta. "How long have you known this girl? How do you know you'll even get along?" I answered her questions with skill, deftly avoiding any verbal pitfalls that would cause her to rescind parental permission to leave the country.

But perhaps I should have heeded the maternal radar for disaster that lay in store for me. An hour after I landed in the Madrid airport, I'd seen a town's worth of raven-haired, green-eyed *mujeres,* but none looking for a lost *americana.*

Then, half an hour after the last of my fellow passengers had drifted away, I finally heard it: "Zhane!" After the previous summer with Marion, I recognized this as a European distortion of "Jenn" and looked up to spy two figures dressed in black striding towards me through the mobs. Marta grabbed both my shoulders and pecked me twice—once on each cheek—as I stood stock still. "We kiss twice in Spain" were her first words to me, spoken matter-of-factly. She then introduced me to Sabina, who greeted me in the same manner, albeit without instruction and more demurely.

Marta had, as she'd described in her letter, shoulder-length black hair, which framed a round face and devilish eyes the color of bright jade. Her raspy voice was assertive, even when she spoke English. In contrast, Sabina, whom I pegged at about 17, a few years younger than both myself and Marta, had a voice as gentle as a grade-school teacher, with a slight touch of naïveté. She seemed comfortably aware that she was playing the part of sidekick.

"How did you know who I was?" I asked Marta, conscious that she'd bee-lined towards me through a crowded international airport.

"Easy," she rasped. "You have 'Made in America' written across your forehead."

Marta's reply struck a blow. Marion had spent the previous summer insisting that, if I visited France, I'd fit in as easily as if I'd been born in a café on the Seine. "You have a European manner," she'd told me, and I'd wanted to believe her with every bone of my Europhile teenage body. I'd even chosen the maroon bodysuit I'd worn on the plane because Marion had declared she had one just like it at home. But despite all my planning, Marta had recognized me among the airport mobs as the lone American. I knew my foreigner status would only become more obvious in situations where I would have to speak Spanish.

Marta had written in her letters that she loved languages and could speak English, German, and Russian, as well as her native Spanish and *Gallego* (Galician), a northwestern Spanish dialect. Her letters had always impressed me with their complexity, especially when I compared her level of English to my level of French. Now, face to face with her, I felt my language-barrier worries dissipate as Marta began to ramble in English—sometimes even with obscure slang—everything she felt it important for me to know: why they were late ("We're Spanish"), how she and Sabina had met, and, most importantly, why I was so damn lucky to be in Spain, the most incredible country on our miserable little rock of a planet. My part of our first face-to-face conversation consisted mostly of nodding and raised eyebrows. For perhaps the first time in my life, I felt myself folding up and tucking away my ego as I slipped into something less comfortable: a submissive role.

For the duration of Marta's introductions, the three of us stood rooted to the same spot in the airport where I'd sat waiting for an hour. From time to time, I flicked my eyes over her shoulder to a clock and couldn't believe that we'd been standing for fifteen minutes without even discussing where we were headed. Marta lived, as I knew from writing her, in León, a town about 210 miles to the north. I'd flown into Madrid on her advice, and she'd promised to escort me to her home, for which I was most grateful. After what seemed like eternity to an impatient New Yorker, my chaperones were ready to leave Barajas Airport.

"Now, where shall we go?" Marta asked. She stood tall and proud, ready to guide me through all the wonders of her capital city—that is, until she attempted to pick up my suitcase and nearly fell over. "What have you in there?" She glanced scornfully at my luggage as if it had just insulted her country.

My face warmed. "Let me handle that." I'd already been pegged as overtly American. I didn't want to complete the stereotype by coming off as a high-maintenance snob who needed to cart her entire boudoir across the ocean. Although my ancient Samsonite suitcase was wheel-less, I had a portable cart to haul it around. As I unfolded the trolley, as Sabina called it, and heaved the suitcase on, I gave a little grunt. "It's the Suitcase From Hell," I explained, managing a meek smile. Marta nodded and, although her eyebrows painted a quizzical expression, she said nothing.

"We have a few hours before our bus." The three of us stepped outdoors into the glaring Spanish sunshine. "Where would you like to go first?"

I looked to Sabina, the native *madrileña* among us. "I have no idea. Where do you suggest?"

The two gave the matter only a moment's thought before exchanging conspiratorial looks. "We know where," Marta said with a grin. "It is a place you know well, I am sure."

I had quite a time getting the Suitcase From Hell off the trolley, onto a bus, then down the subway stairs and through the turnstiles. Marta and Sabina exchanged looks once or twice, and I soldiered on, refusing their attempts to help. I had packed it, I was going to carry it. It had never occurred to me that my suitcase was too large, considering I was planning to stay in Europe for nearly six weeks. To my friends back home on Long Island, a suitcase, small knapsack, and camera bag seemed quite a packing feat for that length of time.

The Suitcase From Hell tried to make amends. On an overcrowded subway car, the three of us found ourselves without seats and we switched off sitting on either end of its hard shell. As Marta and I took our turn, she asked how much Spanish I understood. *"No hablo español"* was my reply and meek attempt at humor.

Marta recoiled as if my breath reeked of garlic—or, worse, a Big Mac. "The grammar is fine," she informed me in her trademark rasp, "but the accent is *horrible."* She went on to explain that, even had my accent been passable, a true Spaniard wouldn't have said *"español"* but rather *"castellano."* Spain was awash with dialects, I was told, and Castilian was both the most common and the preferred dialect of the "more educated" of the masses.

After dragging the Suitcase from the labyrinthine dungeon of the Madrid Metro, we emerged in the Plaza Mayor, a sweeping courtyard ringed by a continuous multi-storied building with innumerable windows. Marta explained that it was one of the premier tourist attractions in Madrid, complete with obligatory cafés, roving herds of young Spaniards, and an equestrian statue of King Felipe III. I was standing in the center of one of Spain's most historic landmarks, she informed me with pride. But that wasn't why she had brought

10

me, as I soon discovered. I wasn't certain, but I had an inkling it had something to do with Depeche Mode.

And there lay the true motive behind my trip to Spain, the reason Marta and I had become friends—all because of four guys from Basildon, England, and a barrage of synthesizers. In early spring, I had written Marta of my plans to visit Marion. She had replied by inviting me to Spain for the two weeks prior to my tour de France, during which she promised we'd see the Spanish stops of their Devotional Tour (named for the most recent album, *Songs of Faith and Devotion*) and possibly—dare I dream it?—meet the band.

Those were the words that had lured me, the words that had burned through her letter as I sat resolutely on the bed in my Long Island home: *meet Depeche Mode.*

For more than five years, my life had revolved around this new wave band that now, in 1993, had only recently become a Top 40 sensation. I'd struck up conversations with strangers because of them, spent thousands of dollars on their merchandise, and fallen in love with a high school boyfriend due to a mutual infatuation with their music. Now I was in Spain to see them in concert with someone I'd met in the pen pal section of *Bong*, the Depeche Mode Fan Club magazine.

I'd hidden much of this information from my parents, my father especially. My mother, however, knew Marta to be a Moder from the intricate devotional drawings that graced the envelopes of her letters. I knew that somehow my mother's hesitation at letting me come to Spain had been partly due to my musical infatuation. I'd had to cover up the fact that I'd been writing to Marta for only a few months, fabricating a multi-year correspondence out of our five or six letters. I conceded some facts to my mom: Marta was indeed a Moder, we would be attending a few concerts, and Marta thought we might be able to (gasp!) meet them. I couldn't contain the excitement in my voice as I related the last part. My mother sighed and shook her head. "Don't be disappointed if that doesn't happen," she said to my glazed, daydreaming eyes. I found my mother's cautioning ironic considering she'd foiled my first chance to meet them, only two years earlier in New York. This time, I vowed, would be different.

"You don't recognize it?" Marta asked, sweeping her arm to indicate the teeming Plaza Mayor.

I took in the scenery. "I think I've seen it in a few textbooks." Truth was, the Plaza Mayor could have been any plaza or piazza or square in Europe, at least as far as an untraveled American-made teenager was concerned. But Marta's nationalistic pride begged a different answer. "I'm sure I've seen it on television once or twice."

As my host rolled her eyes, Sabina tried a different tact. "It's too big, Marta," she said. "Let's show her the *exact place*."

"You're right," said Marta, and her eyes lit up in a way that would soon become all too familiar. "She'll recognize *the sign*."

With Suitcase From Hell in tow, I followed Marta and Sabina across the plaza, drinking in the scenery. Although I wouldn't have designated it a park, especially due to the lack of trees, the plaza was bustling with park-like activities, from teens playing hacky sack to an old man tossing breadcrumbs to pigeons. A handful of cafés were interspersed at various points along the perimeter, and coffee-guzzling patrons clustered around tables, shaded by umbrellas under the orange sky. A few statues were the only permanent fixtures in the otherwise flat landscape, but Marta's doggedness saw us blur right past them. Instead, she headed to the arcade that ringed the whole of the plaza, positioning herself, arms folded, directly below a sign that read: "*Compra—Venta de Sellos Para Collecciones*." The few words I understood on the sign offered no clue as to why this location held any significance. Marta wore a huge grin and looked at me, expecting to see some response. "You recognize it now?"

My heart began to pound. This was a test of some sort, and I was failing it miserably. "I, uh… I have no idea. I'm still really exhausted from the flight and I haven't eaten anything since…"

Marta slapped her arms against her sides in exasperation. "Do you not have the 1991 calendar? The one with Anton's black-and-whites?"

Despite the obscurity of her language, I knew exactly what Marta was referring to. I did indeed have the 1991 Depeche Mode calendar with pictures by Anton Corbijn, but I had no idea what that had to do with the Plaza Mayor.

"Yeah, I have two. One's still in the plastic," I said defensively, hoping this latter fact would attest to my devotion.

"Remember April, the one with Alan and Dave—both our favorites? It was Alan, like this —" and she posed for me, her hands clasped in front of her. "And Dave, like this." She shuffled a few feet to the side and now stood with arms folded. "Both of them looking very serious, like this." Marta's face fell somber for a split second as she channeled the spirits of Alan Wilder and Dave Gahan for her one-person tableau of the April 1991 calendar page. The next moment she was a flurry of movement as her arms insisted I recall the image. *"You don't remember?"*

Even if I hadn't remembered, I would have been unable to admit it. For years I'd known no equal in my love and devotion for the band. No one I'd met at the many concerts and conventions could claim a collection half of what mine was—from colored vinyl to rare international magazines in languages I couldn't even read, from T-shirts of concerts that occurred when I was still in kindergarten to rare bootlegs that weren't even part of the official Depeche Mode canon—if it existed, I *had* to have it. There was no question. I pored through the back pages of *Bong* and the aisles of the various independent record stores of Long Island and Manhattan in search of any Depeche-related trinket I didn't already possess. Nothing was too small (a keychain) or too esoteric (a clipping from a Budapest magazine). On the rare weekend night I didn't go to the alternative nightclub with my friends, I'd stay up until the wee hours of the morning, headphones pushed tightly against my ears in the hopes of discerning every last syllable of their lyrics—British accent be damned—so that I'd have a *complete* binder of their songs. Until that moment in the Plaza Mayor, beads of sweat forming on my forehead as much from the Spanish sun as from the pressure of conjuring the right answer, I had never even considered the possibility that there could be a bigger fan than me.

And I hadn't flown three thousand miles to concede my hard-won throne. "Yeah, now that you mention it. " I fudged some extraneous details so as to appear more convincing. "And Dave was wearing sunglasses, wasn't he?" As if there were more than a dozen photos in the last three years of him without them.

Marta gazed upwards as if she'd been spared a smiting from above. "Thank God," she gasped, serenity returning to her face. "You were beginning to worry me for a moment."

Sabina held my camera bag out towards me, delighted that I'd passed the exam. "Would you like me to take a picture of you two? Just like Dave and Alan?"

As I retrieved my camera from its case, Marta practiced her most Dave-like expressions while Sabina directed. "No, a little less angry. Now move your head to the right. Yes, I think that's it. Now look sexy. You are a sex god! Yes! That's it!"

I received a few tips on posture—and a few more mentions of how American I looked, especially considering I was posing as a Brit—before the picture was finally snapped.

Our shoot over, Marta checked her watch and announced that we had time to grab a bite to eat before the bus to León left. Although my stomach was rumbling like the A train, I dreaded the thought of where we might eat. In my half dozen letters to Marta, I had failed to mention that I was a vegetarian. From the little I'd gleaned from local menus—and Marta's attitude towards those who held beliefs contradictory to hers or her country's—I had the nagging feeling that a meat-free regime was not looked upon favorably in Spain, especially by my host. Without much fanfare, I managed to order a *bocadillo con queso*, a Spanish cheese sandwich on bread so hard my gums bled. After lunch, Marta and I bid *adiós* to Sabina, with whom we'd meet up again for the Madrid concert, and departed for the bus station.

Once aboard, fatigue overtook me and I was asleep before the wheels had started rolling. Every so often I'd open my eyes to take in the scenery. For the most part, the region we passed through was flat, allowing for views for miles in every direction. Fatigue may have distorted my memory, but I recall the land as being a warm, dusty red that seemed to overtake every aspect of the landscape down to the trees, which were stumpy and clustered together in sporadic groupings that probably passed for a forest in that region, even though a sidewalk in Times Square contained more foliage. The trees themselves were crooked little twigs with no undergrowth beneath them, only a small cluster stuck in the middle of the flat, barren redness. In the distance squatted small mountains, mere hills of rock that jutted out for the sole purpose of creating obstacles in our path. From miles away you could see the dust of an approaching vehicle, which usually took longer than necessary to pass due to the excessive contortions of the road.

As the sun began to set, I exhaled a breath of exhaustion that the day had finally come to a close. I guessed the time at somewhere around 8:30 and was shocked when I looked at my watch and found it two hours later than that. *The sun sets later in Spain,* I mused. *No wonder they need siestas in the afternoon.*

I must have dozed off to the drone of the dubbed Harrison Ford movie because I woke to the touch of a hand on my chin and found Marta trying to close my gaping mouth. I hid my mortification by turning to the side and going back to sleep for a few hours until I felt the bus lurch to a stop.

We'd pulled up to a roadside *cafetería,* the Spanish equivalent of a greasy spoon in which I would find myself quite often over the next week. As the entire bus debarked and entered the squat wooden structure, I finally felt the miles that separated me from my home. Though on a smaller scale, Madrid had been too much like New York for me to comprehend that, after all my years of dreaming, I had finally reached Europe—albeit a Europe that more closely resembled how I'd pictured Mexico.

The cafetería was the only object taller than a person that I could see in any direction. As I pushed aside the curtain of beads that hung in the doorway of the establishment, I felt as if I'd been immersed in Spain. The inside buzzed with the hungry native tongues ordering Oranginas, *cafés,* bocadillos, and other Spanish mainstays. I was too tired to eat. I used the bathroom—and, in doing so, discovered that the Spanish concept of toilet paper was quite different than the American—and returned to the bus with Marta, who had spoken fewer than two sentences to me since leaving the capital.

Lost in the middle of the desolate red landscape, a wave of isolation swept over me. Whenever I'd hole myself up in my bedroom, my padded headphones promising isolation from the outside world, I'd welcomed the seclusion, the disconnectedness, even as the band's music united me with the myriad other souls strewn across the globe who I knew, just *knew*, were performing the same ritual in their own homes. But there in the middle of the barren Spanish topography, I couldn't escape the isolation with the press of an "off" button. In my search for kindred souls, I'd managed to detach myself from all familiar connections. But the thought didn't unnerve. In fact, I relished the sense of adventure, especially since any warning signs I'd yet seen were rather innocuous.

When we arrived in León two hours later, I finally began to comprehend the situation I had gotten myself into.

Marta's friend met us at the bus station. During the ride, she had mentioned the possibility of our staying the night at Julio's, not at her home, due to some little untruth she'd told before leaving to collect me. I soon learned that Marta had not been entirely factual with her parents about our itinerary of following our idols across Spain, as she had led me to believe. While we were in Madrid, Marta's parents weren't even aware that I had arrived; in fact, they believed that Marta was visiting a friend for a few days before picking me up and delivering me straight to the Paredes family abode three days hence. The purpose of all this was to allow me and Marta the time to attend the first concert on the west coast of Spain, then return home before the Madrid show, which her parents knew we would be attending with Sabina and Estevo, Marta's younger brother.

Marta had arranged for us to stay at Julio's the night before we left on our adventure so that I could drop off the bulk of my luggage. But after giving the matter additional thought, she decided that I would be better off in a hotel since she had several errands to run for school early the next morning. I tried to convince Marta that I truly wouldn't mind staying at her friend's while she was out, but she knew better.

"You are tired, yes? You will enjoy catching up on sleep in a hotel," she informed me. "You look like you need some sleep."

Despite my genetically imposed frugality, I agreed. The last thing I wanted was to start my trip off with a fight. The first thing I wanted was a bed.

When I woke the next day, I began the morning trying to convince myself that I hadn't been rash when I'd accepted a stranger's invitation to a foreign country. Adventuresome was more like it. Surely Marta would be back soon because it was already eleven—almost time to check out, which she well knew. After a refreshing shower and the realization that I'd forgotten to pack toothpaste, which caused me great consternation as I couldn't consider myself completely awake without a minty-fresh mouth, I poked my head outside my room. The chambermaid, going about her daily rounds, greeted me warmly. *"¡Buenas días, señorita!"* I smiled and decided to test my Spanish on the poor unsuspecting woman.

Since I hadn't learned the word for "toothpaste" in any of my Spanish classes, I called upon a lesson from my eighth-grade Spanish teacher and rattled off a few common American brands with a Spanish inflection. I soon got my point across with shockingly little trouble when I hit upon *Colgate* (COAL-ga-tay) and felt a smug satisfaction at my resourcefulness. Moments later, I was running my tongue across clean teeth with satisfaction.

At a little after the imposed checkout time, I dragged my luggage down to the lobby. There was a slight vocabulary struggle with the concierge, but I managed to convey to him that I didn't know where my *amiga* was and that I couldn't possibly slum around León with a suitcase the size of Catalonia. Accustomed to receiving a less-than-gracious New York attitude when dealing with those in the lower rungs of customer service, I was pleasantly surprised when the concierge offered to watch my bags so that I could take in the sites of León until Marta returned. *"León es una cuidad hermosa!"* he said as he bade me to take in some fresh air. I told him I would be down by the river (perhaps working the banks, considering my poor Spanish) and he nodded, waving me out as if I hadn't showered and was stinking up the place.

I could actually feel my eyes strain from dilation as I stepped into the daylight. Perhaps spending the majority of my summer days cooped up in a downtown office and my nights in clubs had made my eyes unaccustomed to the severe brightness, but the sheer blinding power of the Spanish sun would become as much a part of my memory of my trip as the various forms of transportation, bocadillos, and frantic quests for backstage passes. When I'd met her at the airport, in addition to informing me of my glaring American-ness, Marta had declared that I was in dire need of a tan. As the sunlight scorched my pasty skin, I doubted I'd leave sun-kissed. Parboiled was more like it.

Hotel Ríosol, where I had spent my first-ever night outside of North America, was situated on the outskirts of León. The center of town was located across one of the many old stone bridges that breached the small trickle of a river, near which I planted myself and began scribbling away in my diary while baring my white legs in offering to the sun.

I'd kept a journal since I was in kindergarten. Volumes of self-important confessions sat locked away in my steamer trunk back home. Now, sitting on the banks of a foreign river, I spelled out all my misgivings—how I wasn't sure if I could trust Marta, how I'd left matters with my parents, and what the hell I'd do if my friends found out the transgression I'd committed only days before I'd left. As vulnerable as I felt, spilling my guts kept me grounded and helped me forget that I may have already been abandoned by the one person I knew in this far-off land.

I looked up from time to time to spy a passing Spanish gentleman giving me a once-over, and I recalled both Marta's words of how obviously American I looked and my ninth-grade Spanish teacher's quips about the "friendliness" of the Spanish, especially the men. Ms. O'Farrell had told me enough times that my red hair would be quite an attraction overseas, especially in Italy and on the Iberian Peninsula. I was only just beginning to find this out firsthand.

Several times I was approached by someone offering a kind "hello," to which I responded with the appropriate and foolproof *"hola."* But when the men, who ranged in age from about twelve to fifty-five, reached the point of striking up a full-fledged conversation, I would shrug and say, *"Lo siento. No hablo español."* This usually encouraged them to try their hands at English or, much to my relief, to tip their hats and be on their way.

I'd endured about five such encounters before I heard a familiar raspy voice, and felt both relief and apprehension. Marta's shadow fell over my diary and, after a quick dismissal of her lateness, she introduced me to her cousin Cynthia, who was visiting from Seville. Cynthia spoke worse English than I spoke Spanish, and both of our mutual accents were so horrible that we couldn't begin to communicate in our common language of French. We soon gave up and turned to Marta whenever we wanted to speak, unwittingly empowering our translator. If I asked Cynthia a question, Marta would pause several seconds before deigning to answer, holding her power of communication over our heads as if she had her finger resting on the Soviets' Big Red Button.

Cynthia was the complete opposite of Marta. While her cousin had adopted a fashion sense that could have been called Gothic Lite, Cynthia was a cheery, ever-smiling sidekick whose closet most likely accepted black garments only out of funereal necessity. The two of them huddled together for a few moments, and I was able to glean that they were deciding which parts of León to show me. "Do you like cathedrals?" Marta finally asked me, almost as an afterthought. "We will take you to one. It is beautiful. You will love it."

Her statement left little room for disagreement. I knew that even if I'd told her I was half Jewish and didn't care much for cathedrals, it wouldn't have fazed my host any more than if I'd said I was a direct descendent of the Pope. I was to witness this same conversational pattern over the course of our travels: a question where I thought I had a chance to respond, a statement where I learned otherwise, and the declaration that I would, without a doubt, love the Spanish icon in question.

After the long trip through the flatlands of Spain, the quaint metropolis of León was a more than welcome sight. Marta and Cynthia led me across a bridge to the center of town and through the narrow cobbled streets. I hardly understood anything that passed between the two cousins, particularly anything that came out of Cynthia's mouth. Marta soon explained that southerners from Cynthia's region dropped most of their "S's," causing *"español"* to be pronounced *"epañol."* Though I didn't understand Marta's Spanish much better—her Uzi-rapid speech, gravelly voice, and tutored British accent sometimes made understanding her English a challenge—I could still comprehend enough to notice the difference, and to aid Marta in mocking her cousin's speech.

As we wandered through town, Marta pointed out interesting historical tidbits behind the sites, including how León had been the capital of Spain hundreds of years earlier and why the capital had since been moved to Madrid. Her nationalistic pride and caustic feelings for the Catalan region to the east wove themselves throughout her speech. Cynthia seemed to agree on most every aspect, though Marta remained the most vocal, expressing what appeared to be a "true" Spaniard's (as opposed to a Catalan's) opinions on the relation between the two Iberian regions.

Marta often repeated her dislike for Catalonia, how the rivalry with Spain had been further fueled a few years back when the Olympics had been hosted in the Catalan city of Barcelona. The Spanish king, she explained, had been faced with the difficult decision of choosing which language he should use to greet the world at the opening ceremonies. Marta seemed to support his choice to speak the opening few words in Catalan before switching over to "true" Spanish. She smiled proudly, a glint in her eyes. "He is a good king."

A moment later, her hands firmly planted on her hips like a conquistador, she declared, "We will go to Catalan for the final concert. It will be difficult, yes, because I do not speak Catalan. They do not like when we speak Spanish. There is a great rivalry, and they will pretend not to understand. It is a shame because Barcelona is so beautiful." She turned and tried her hypnotic powers on me. "Are you looking forward to going? It is not as beautiful as our city of Madrid, but it is nice, Barcelona. When we have seen both cities, you will see how much more wonderful Madrid is. It is the *puta madre*. You will love it."

I nodded and continued trudging along through the sun-soaked streets. I had left my luggage at the hotel after Marta assured me that the concierge would not mind if we returned for it later, and even though I was worried about my belongings, I was glad to not have the burden of the Suitcase From Hell. Marta had pointed to the river as we crossed the bridge and informed me that, had my suitcase been with us at that moment, she would surely have tossed it over. "But I still have your copy of *Dracula* in there." I refrained from telling her that I'd purchased the copy from a black-market vendor in Chinatown.

"The Suitcase From Hell should go back to hell," she said simply. "After I get my movie, of course."

In comparison to my brief tour of Madrid, I found the simplicity of Marta's town—not her hometown, I was often reminded, but where she currently lived—refreshing. It was just as I had pictured: tapered alleys lined with tall stone buildings with shuttered windows and potted plants; small cars with elongated license plates and frantic drivers frustrated with the ever-present traffic circles; ancient fountains surrounded by red-nosed old men sipping from wine bottles hidden in brown paper bags. We passed a park on the way to the cathedral and I heard a strange shrieking cry.

"It is a bird," Marta told me when I asked. "I do not know the name in English. It is a big bird."

I tried to imagine what sort of "big birds" lived in Spain and decided not to tell Marta that I was distantly related (only by marriage) to Big

Bird, of Muppets fame. That would have been too gauchely American. "Big as in bigger than a parakeet," I asked, "or big as in mini-van big?"

Marta shrugged again. "Big. Like this." She held her hand about three feet off the ground.

"Yeah, that's a big bird," I nodded. "A turkey, perhaps?"

"Turkey?" Marta contemplated the word and deemed it sizeable enough to define her large Spanish fowl. "Yes, a turkey. That is what you hear. But come, the birds are boring. The cathedral you will love." She then added the common Spanish phrase I would come to learn meant "the very best," despite its literal translation, "mother whore": "It is the *puta madre* of all Spanish cathedrals."

The structure Marta described soon loomed above the buildings that surrounded us. I had seen only two true cathedrals in my life, St. Patrick's in Manhattan and the one near my Long Island hometown. I had often walked around the Garden City Cathedral on sunny days when I needed an escape and couldn't imagine a more beautiful structure until I'd visited St. Patrick's. Both paled in comparison to the sight I beheld on that street in León.

Up until then, I'd felt an enormous sense of guilt over the amount of money my parents had spent sending me to Europe. I thought of my father's pride and excitement as he talked about my trip. "I want this for you more than you can imagine," he'd said to me one night, his eyes brighter than usual after a day of work. "This experience will help you to grow more than any of the academic summer programs I've paid for throughout the years. You'll improve your French, see foreign cities, meet new people, and visit historic sites that I've only dreamed of!" But when I'd stepped on the plane only two days earlier, none of my father's dreams for me had meant anything. They were his dreams, something as foreign as the Galician language being spoken around me.

All I had been able to think of were the concerts Marta had promised I would see. And that I would meet Depeche Mode.

But when I entered the cathedral, I forgot all the other reasons that had brought me to Europe. It wasn't simply the beauty and intricacy that flowed over the entire surface of the building but the tales that came with it. As I touched the carved stone, I thought of the years of history it had seen, the centuries the cathedral had endured, and how the town about it had changed into something that hardly resembled what had been there when the first brick had been laid centuries earlier. Nothing back on my continent came close to the age of the building that Marta visited on a near-daily basis.

I brushed my fingertips against the brick. "Six hundred years old," Marta said, my voiceover guide. "It is beautiful, yes? There is nothing like it in all the country. And it is here in León." She beamed with pride.

We walked the cathedral's corridors, I with my head tilted back in awe the greater part of the time, eyes lifted to the vaulted ceiling and its intricate patterns. The sun filtered through the stained-glass windows in a single ray of light that shone as a yellow patch on the floor. I listened to the sound of my footsteps on the stone, trying to imagine how many others had passed through here over the ages and from how many different cultures. I gazed through the bars into the tombs where candles burned in honor of the bishops who lay buried there. Though I'd never been remotely religious—unless you counted my stint in kindergarten Bible school when I had a crush on Bobby Strider and his Star Wars figurine collection—I suddenly found myself captivated by the aura of the place, the history, faith, and determination that had built the walls and kept the cathedral alive over the years, the unadulterated devotion.

Marta pointed to a statue in one of the rooms off to the side. She explained that during the week of Easter, the *Semana Santa,* she and other members of her church's "brotherhood" carried the statue of Mary on a *paso*—which Marta translated as a "step" but was really more of a human-powered float—through the streets of the city. In addition to the immense weight of the statue on their backs, the members wore long, heavy-hooded robes, the uniforms of their brotherhood, to hide their identities. For the female members, anonymity was especially important, Marta told me, because a great many of the males believed that, per tradition, the *pasos* should not be carried by women. She explained that one year after having carried the step, the brotherhood removed their hoods. When the young man who had been walking next to Marta discovered he had completed his sacred duty at the side of a female, he called her a bitch straight to her face. "It is very hard," she said, shaking her head. "They make it so hard for us. We try and we do as well as them, but it is the tradition that makes them prejudiced against us. It is not fair. Not fair at all."

Although I couldn't empathize with the dogma, I completely understood Marta's plight in a sexist situation. What made it doubly confounding to me, however, was that Marta and the rest of her step-carrying posse were all of the same faith and, therefore, should have considered each other equals. I couldn't comprehend ascribing to a religion of any sort—I'd ditched Bible school when Bobby Strider moved to Kentucky—let alone one where I wasn't considered an equal.

I stared intently at the statue of Mary, trying to imagine how it would feel hauling a gargantuan sacred artifact on my back. As with most every aspect of her culture, Marta took great pride in her brotherhood, and I couldn't think of anything in my life that compared. It was something she believed in and felt strongly enough about to risk ridicule and undergo physically demanding ordeals. The closest experience I'd had to that was gym class.

We left the cool darkness of the cathedral to return to the severity of the Spanish sunlight. "You will not be white when you leave Spain," Marta promised as she pressed a finger to my skin and watched as it appeared white in comparison to the red region around it. "Though I think you may need some suntan lotion."

We enjoyed a drink at the outdoor café in front of the cathedral, taking shelter from the heat underneath the umbrellas. Marta asked what kind of car I drove. When I told her a 1980 Firebird, she considered this at length.

"Do you have specialty license plates? You know, the kind with your own message?"

Cynthia leaned in, as if the whole of America's reputation depended on this one answer. "Vanity plates?" I said. "No, standard state-issued. Why?"

Marta sighed and leaned back in her chair, which Cynthia took as a good omen. "The last American who visited me was one of your stereotypes, the ones we Spanish *hate*. She had a sports car with vanity plates. And she was a cheerleader. Needless to say, we did not get along."

I considered Marta's response and decided now was not the time to tell her I was in a sorority, a sisterhood worlds apart from her brotherhood. Instead, I opted for flattering my host. "You know, visiting that cathedral alone was well worth my trip to Spain." Marta translated my praise to Cynthia. "I've never touched something so old. There's nothing on my continent on such a grand scale that comes close to it. I can't wait to tell my father. This is exactly the kind of thing he wanted me to experience."

Without even looking in her direction, I could feel the waves of pride swelling off my Spanish host. Even as I spoke my words, I felt a pang of guilt at the thought of my father. Despite our emotional gap—or perhaps in an attempt to breach it—I told Marta why.

Before leaving for Europe, one of the Twelve Apostles—the moniker my musically addicted high school friends had dubbed ourselves—had visited me in my Manhattan apartment and, with the help of our fake IDs, we'd painted the town—or at least the Village—goth black, knocking back potent potables well into the night. Our livers declared a truce just as the sun threatened to crack the horizon, and so we ventured back uptown. Unfortunately, we didn't hear the subway announcement that our train had changed from a local to an express. Sebastian and I discovered this when we sped past my stop at 81st and watched as the street numbers continued to climb into the triple digits.

"Jenn, where are we?"

As the train slowed at 125th Street, I shot him a smile to mask my own anxiety and pulled him onto the platform. "Harlem." In 1993, before the neighborhood's gentrification, the name still signified a touch of gamble, particularly for young white suburbanites trying to pass themselves off as urban sophisticates.

We stood at the stop for several minutes waiting for the downtown local train. To pass the time, we each lit a cigarette, though I hardly ever smoked. "This is crazy," Sebastian said. Then with an impish grin, he added, "Something like this would only happen with you. Harlem subway station at 3:30 am. Sheesh."

"Wait," I said, cocking my head in the direction of two approaching police officers. "It gets better. Put out your cigarette."

Sebastian and I got off relatively easy, I told Marta. Considering we each were underage, carrying alcohol, had fake IDs, and were slightly tipsy—and that Sebastian was carrying a rather large knife—the $50 tickets we received for smoking were a blessing.

Until my father found mine.

The morning I was leaving for Europe, my father approached me. Though I felt guilty doing so, I told him some convoluted lie that acquitted me of being a smoker. He accepted without further questioning and left for work shortly thereafter. By the time I'd finished packing, the guilt had fully kicked in. Moments later, I was speeding across town in my Firebird to fess up.

It was early afternoon at Gum Ying, the Chinese restaurant and bar that served as my father's other office. The off-peak hour meant we had the place to ourselves, once Dad had dismissed "Uncle" Louie the bartender. A single beam of sunlight illuminated the bar while my father digested the information that his daughter had both lied to him and was a smoker. I could almost hear the many cogs, well greased by gin and tonics, whir inside his head. After a moment, he sighed and held up his own pack of Winstons, the jowls on his face sagging more than usual.

"I can't get mad at you for something I do myself," he said. His dismissal seemed too easy, and I hoped that he wouldn't bring up the fact that, just a few years earlier, I'd made it my mission to hide his cigarettes whenever he came home. At my sister's wedding, my father and I had stood before the chuppah, indulging in nostalgic reverie. He was smoking, despite the venue's ordinances against doing so, and I snatched the cigarette from his lips. I was only in ninth grade, my sister eleven years older than me, but I was forever planning ahead.

"Dad," I said with solemnity, hoping my bridesmaid's garb imparted more authority than someone my age demanded, "I want you to be here for *my* wedding." I stubbed out the cigarette and kicked it under the aisle runner.

"I will be," he said, already reaching inside his tuxedo jacket for another pack. "I will be. And your wedding will be even bigger than this!" He threw open his arms as if to embrace the whole of the castle, then quickly lit another smoke.

Whether or not my father recalled any of the impromptu anti-smoking PSAs I had produced over the past decade, the realization that I too was now a smoker probably caused him not a small twinge of guilt.

He waggled a fleshy finger inches from my face. "As long as you're not smoking any of those funny cigarettes." His eyes bulged with intensity. Had it not been for his conviction, his reprimand would have been humorous, especially with his jowls flapping as they did. My father might have been a smoker and semi-functional alcoholic, as were many men of his generation, but the idea of illicit drugs repulsed him.

I assured him that I was not a pothead and he exhaled in relief. After only moments, he seemed to resign himself to the newfound knowledge about his youngest daughter, and I felt that this minor incident had somehow brought us closer together, as much due to honesty as our now mutual vice. When I boarded the plane later that day, a tight wad of money from Dad sitting in my pocket, I felt some relief, some solace—not to mention resolve that I was on the right path and that my quest to meet the band would be fulfilled.

Marta, on the other hand, hadn't thought twice about lying to her parents. As we sat drinking our overpriced Coca-Colas, she explained her game plan. "We will leave tonight on the train to Pontevedra, my hometown. I am Galician." She lisped the "c" as a "th"—*Galithian*—in typical Castilian style. "You will be visiting my true home, so we won't need a map. I love León, yes, but Pontevedra is where my heart lies." She glanced around the plaza, a satisfied expression showing below her ultra-dark sunglasses. "We will leave very late, I think. Yes, very late. The concert is tomorrow night. We will return here to León the day after and my parents will never know. You will meet them and they will think you have only just arrived. Perfect! Then we will go to Madrid with my brother to see the next show. I don't know how we will see the Barcelona show yet, but I will think of a way." She leaned back, her forehead creased in deep concentration. "Yes, I will think of a way."

Marta went on to explain that she had the largest collection of Depeche Mode paraphernalia in all of León, possibly even all of Spain. I didn't quite believe her until she began to name all the different items she owned. I'd thought my own collection impressive when I estimated it to be worth roughly $4,000, but with what Marta described to me, it was a safe estimate that hers was worth at least four times that. I couldn't wait for my formal León homecoming, when her parents would officially know I'd arrived, so that I could copy some of her songs and articles. Sabina had mentioned the day before that I would soon see just how big a fan Marta actually was, that her faith and devotion for Depeche almost outweighed that for her brotherhood. "It is as another religion for her, Zhane," she told me in confidence, almost able to pronounce my name. Marta's elaborate schemes to attend every concert in Spain attested to that fact.

Later in the day, we returned to the Hotel Ríosol to retrieve my belongings. Reunited with the Suitcase From Hell and all the problems that accompanied it, Marta and I fell into our now-old routine of pulling, carrying, and complaining. We took a taxi to Julio's house on the other side of town, where I was told I would be leaving my bags until Marta and I returned from Pontevedra. I didn't think twice about leaving the majority of my personal and important belongings with a near total stranger, mainly because I had little choice. I had gotten myself into this situation and had no one to blame for it but myself. My only options were to do as Marta said or to flee for France a few weeks ahead of time and pray that Marion's family would offer refuge. But I've never been one to take the low-risk alternative, partly because I rarely look far enough ahead into the future to see which outcome I might prefer. Not to mention the fact that giving up on my quest to meet the band was not an option.

Before I'd left for Europe, my eldest sister, Janys, had given me a slightly belated (about five months late) birthday present, a brown leather backpack that I now began to fill with items for the next two days. Marta, Cynthia, and Julio looked on as I fit one item after another into the bag.

"Zhane," Marta said, "it is for only two days, not two years."

I thought for a second, then shrugged. "Better to be safe than sorry. And it's not that heavy anyway." I lifted the bag with one hand to demonstrate.

"Yes, but we will move a lot, do a lot of walking." Marta shimmied to demonstrate the concept of movement. I found her pantomimes amusing and refrained from reminding her that, since English was my native language, they weren't necessary. "You will not want such a heavy bag as this."

I envisioned myself schlepping the bag in the heat. "You're right. I'll repack."

"Wake me when you're done." Marta pretended to doze off on Julio's shoulder, then roused herself to remind me that our train would be leaving a little after midnight and promptly excused herself.

A few moments later, I had narrowed down my items to four shirts, five days' worth of underwear, two pairs of shorts, my journal, address book, camera, and some stationery. Marta returned to inform me, in a voice that was not overly chipper, that she and Cynthia would be returning to her house for a bit, just to settle a few issues with her parents, but that she would be right back. Poor Julio acquired the job of entertaining me—not an easy task considering the deficiency we had in each other's language.

We spent the next two hours swapping music—I introduced him to Toad the Wet Sprocket and Rosetta Stone while he tried to change my unfaltering distaste for Bruce Springsteen. I tried to explain New York's disdain for all things New Jersey, even likening it to Castile vs. Catalonia, but for Julio, the Boss could do no wrong, no matter that he hailed from the armpit of America. Julio then showed me the lyrics to "Red Headed Woman," smiling warmly until I helped translate the slang he had thought referred to a sweet-natured girlfriend but which I read as more of an homage to a slut. I laughed it off, but Julio was so embarrassed by his gaffe that he was still apologizing when Marta returned, without Cynthia. The look on her face did not bode well.

"It is time. We are going," she said curtly. I took it that things had not gone as planned at Casa Paredes. I thanked Julio and his mother quickly for their hospitality before Marta and I were off once again.

Night had already fallen upon León as we walked the deserted streets of her town, one bag apiece slung on our backs. It felt odd, yet relieving, to have left the Suitcase From Hell behind.

I tried asking what had happened at her home and, after a deep breath, my host sighed. "I have been kicked out of my house again."

The first part of the sentence had been bad enough, but at the mention of the word "again," my stomach dropped somewhere down near my ankles. How many times had Marta been "kicked out" of her house? And for what reasons? Was it her or her parents? I didn't know what would be worse, traveling through a foreign country with a juvenile delinquent or returning home to said delinquent's sadistic parents. I briefly considered giving up on the Depeche Mode jaunt altogether and jumping on the next flight to France, where at least I knew level-headed Marion. My parents would probably feel happier knowing I wasn't romping across Iberia with someone they'd never met, and I'd feel safer for the next few weeks knowing that I hadn't put my life in the hands of a psychotic new-wave groupie.

But I quickly dispelled those thoughts. I had come so far already, and the thought of meeting the band eclipsed any worries I might—or should—have had. We walked along, from time to time gazing up at the stars. They were so much brighter than back home, where the Manhattan lights drowned out all possibility of spotting any celestial body other than Northwest Airlines. The Spanish air was fresh and clean, and I felt safe as we meandered toward the train station, even though the dimly lit streets were eerily vacant.

I had written letters to Marta for about a year—six letters at most. It's true that we seemed to hold more in common than I did with my various other pen pals, but personality quirks tend to trump common interests, especially on the road. Luckily, Marta and I had no great conflicts as of yet, excepting the possibility of my anger towards her lying. She seemed sincere enough when we spoke of personal matters, though most conversations tended toward her infatuation with Dave Gahan, our favorite band's lead singer. She spoke of the time she had met him and how she'd had to use every ounce of willpower to control her actions. "Why are your hands behind your back? Let me see your hands," he had said to her.

She revealed them quickly then hid them again. "It is better if I stand like this," she'd told him, insinuating with her eyes and tone of voice that, were legal ramifications not a high probability, she'd have jumped his bones right there.

In spite of my disdain for their overt groupie-ness, I was jealous of her stories, the fact that she had met our mutual idols and held actual conversations with them. "They are like friends," she had told me in one of her letters, and I had felt the greatest green surge of envy seethe within. I would soon discover just how true her words were.

Our train didn't leave for another hour, so Marta and I hiked across a street under construction—one in such upheaval that I wondered if I weren't in the midst of the Croatian war—in order to reach Marta's favorite cafetería. The menu seemed chock full of fabulous dishes—fabulous, that is, if you were a carnivore, which I wasn't. About the only vegetarian items that seemed safe were a salad and an order of fries.

I quickly learned that the Spanish concept of salad differed greatly from the American version. The cook tossed together all manner of vegetables with vinegar and egg. I picked at my meal, wishing all the time that I had ordered another damn bocadillo. My only consolation was that the *patatas fritas* were absolutely delicious, especially with the creamy garlic sauce on the side for dipping.

As we were leaving, the man behind the counter called us back and attempted conversation with me. Marta jumped in and explained that I spoke very little Spanish, then informed me that the man was wondering why I had barely touched his salad, "the best salad in all of León." When he heard me try to explain that I was American, unused to Spanish food and a vegetarian to boot, he laughed and, at hearing me praise his country, gifted me the local equivalent of a Hostess cake. The incident taught me a lesson I would take with me through subsequent travels: Complimenting the natives on their homeland often results in a reward, usually in the form of food.

When the train pulled into the station, Marta double-checked the cars several times for signs before climbing aboard. Midway through the night, the train would split and half the cars would go to one city, half to another. If we weren't careful, we might board a car to Portugal.

I suppose our luck was running rather thin that day because our train was overbooked. Without seats, we were forced to stand in the breezy corridor near the entrance of the train, about two feet from the rather fragrant bathrooms. The train heaved forward, and into the darkness of night we slid along the rails.

I was exhausted once again, more mentally than physically. I sat on the drafty floor and leaned my head back against the wall. It was going to be another long night.

3

"Wake up, Zhane. We are changing cars." Marta shook my shoulder roughly as I opened my eyes. I checked my watch. I'd been asleep an entire fifteen minutes.

"Why? What's going on?"

Marta cocked her head in the direction of the hallway in front of the compartments. "There are angry men. It is not a good situation for two girls traveling alone. Come. We are going." I reluctantly left the warm spot I'd created for myself. The underside of my body that had been in contact with the wall and floor felt exceptionally cold, and I shivered as a chill passed down my spine.

I glanced through the sliding glass door that separated the hallway in front of the compartments from the area where Marta, myself, and several other seatless passengers stood about. Several men—one of whom seemed to wear a uniform of authority—were arguing. A younger man, who looked thoroughly perplexed, kept repeating over and over again, "I don't speak Spanish! I can't understand what you're saying!" I glanced at Marta.

"He understands," she whispered. "He just doesn't want to pay the fare."

We gathered our bags and crossed between the cars, where we stayed only a few moments before the younger man entered and walked briskly past us. Marta's eyes followed him, then widened with a twitch of her eyebrow. "Not bad. He can come back if he likes."

I nodded in agreement. "Kind of a California look to him. Definitely not bad."

The fare-hopper muttered aloud to himself as he passed through. When I thought the doors had closed behind him, I turned to Marta. "Australian," I said with an air of authority. Finally, I could have the upper hand on language. "He's Australian."

"Am not!" I turned to find the subject of my conversation leaning through the doorway. For a moment I was at a loss for words. "New Zealand, actually." And with that, the traveler joined me and Marta in our luxurious accommodations on the floor. Although we never learned his name, despite listening to his stories the better part of four hours, Marta and I later came to refer to him as "Kiwi," and we cared little how derogatory the moniker might be. We soon learned that Kiwi had left his home in New Zealand three years earlier with his bike to begin his travels across the world. In all that time, he hadn't once been back home, but he had seen more of this world than most people knew existed.

Meeting him seemed to me an omen, a sign of what my next step should be—whether it was next semester or after graduation, I didn't know. But I envied him, I knew that much. He was living the life that I lived every night when I fell asleep. And here I was just venturing out into that dream, awakened for the first time. I wanted this life, apprehension be damned. Marta might have been presumptuous when she lied to her parents without first filling me in on her plan, but I'd since bought a ticket and was along for the ride. My three days abroad couldn't compare to Kiwi's three years, but I was on my way, albeit bipedal instead of by pedal.

Kiwi informed us that he was on his way to Portugal with a goal of biking down the coast before moving on across the strait to Morocco. In the middle of relating his adventures, he was interrupted by the train conductor, who informed us that a compartment had opened up and that we were welcome to take the seats there. As I stood up, I noted that I had lost all sense of feeling in my toes, though whether it was due to the cold or the fact that Kiwi's bag had been lying on my legs and cutting off circulation for half an hour, I didn't know.

Marta sprawled out on one of the long four-person seats, leaving the other for me and our new acquaintance. Kiwi told me to lie down, that he was used to sleeping upright. I was too tired to argue and did as I was told. Moments later, I was off to slumberland. When I awoke sometime during the night to Marta telling me that the trains were splitting and that we were on the wrong one, Kiwi was gone.

Although Marta and I quickly managed to hop aboard the correct car, we soon found ourselves seatless again. "This is Tuesday the 13th," she declared. We stood in the last car, in the same uncomfortably frigid area as when we first left León.

"I wonder if Dave will still have his hair long," she mused. Her face grew more serious as she pondered this most important of questions. I knew without her having to say so that she was referring to David Gahan, who had, since the last album, changed his appearance from clean-cut Basildon boy to unbathed grunge god. "No, he will not have cut it," she assured herself. "He is gorgeous with his hair—and those tattoos! Although I do not like that he thinks he is Jesus." At least we agreed there. As lead singer, Dave definitely commanded the lion's share of female adoration, and he displayed his gratitude onstage and in videos with sacrilegious posturing—arms outstretched, head bowed yet still swaying with the rhythm—as his acolytes roared their allegiance.

Although an ever faithful, card-carrying Devotee, as some Moders had taken to calling themselves after the release of *Songs of Faith and Devotion,* I had never belonged to the Dave fan camp. This was partially due to my distaste for bravado and partially because of my aversion to convention: With a few possible exceptions in music history, the lead singer of any band has always been the fan fave, and, as with other areas in my life, I preferred to devote my esteem to the underdog.

"Oh, what I wouldn't let that man do to me," Marta sighed, her eyes drifting heavenwards. "Who is your favorite, Zhane?"

It was a question I'd been dreading, not simply because of my answer but because of the very nature of the question. Despite my undying love for the band, I didn't share Marta's feelings. Sure, Dave had his allure, but hot sex gods weren't what had made me spend hours alone in my room, headphones clamped tightly over my ears as I studied each individual word and electronic chirp. For me, my infatuation had always been about the music, and while I knew that Marta knew every song as well—probably better, since she'd had to battle the language barrier—as I did, her question made me all too aware of the divide between us, one that has existed between female music aficionados since the Beatles landed at JFK.

I'd long since developed an aversion to shrill-voiced female "fans" who doted on the musicians more than they did the music. I associated such adoration with that usually bestowed upon fabricated boy bands and acts like Milli Vanilli. True music fans did not cheapen the significance of the music by swooning over shirtless singers and tatted drummers.

This fact had been instilled in me by my sister Janys, who had for years kept an altar to Peter Frampton. When I was born, Janys' personal domain had been significantly diminished with the erection of a wall that partitioned her room into two: one large L-shaped area for her, a shoebox of space for her newborn, 11-years-younger sister. My parents quickly went about gussying up my new abode with hot pink paint and dolly wallpaper, while Janys' realm went largely untouched, mainly at her insistence, and she proceeded to decorate her barren side of the drywall with posters and teenage graffiti denoting her favorite bands. Over the years, the scrawlings she and her friends produced covered the entire side of the room. The Wall became a revered piece of my sister's musical history.

While I was still in grade school, Janys covered a large portion of the indoor street art with a poster, which she framed with colored tinfoil stars and topped off with a red-glitter bubble-letter marquee that screamed, "Frampton!" For years, part of her bedtime ritual—and mine, when she had babysitting duties—was to light a candle, play a Frampton track (I always requested the "talking guitar song"), then kiss the poster goodnight before falling asleep to the sound of the hi-fi needle nestling into the center of the album.

By the time the early '80s rolled around and my purple-haired sister entered high school, Frampton had been replaced by the Grateful Dead, David Bowie, and a mishmash of rock stars more befitting a matured teen than did a baby-faced pretty boy. I glanced at a band shot of the Dead and couldn't imagine Jerry Garcia receiving a goodnight kiss from my sister. "It's not about the looks. It's about the *music.* Remember that," she admonished.

Even though neither Bowie nor Garcia received the tinfoil-star-and-glitter treatment, the former went on to hold a prominence for me that Frampton never did. I watched my sister sop her head with fuchsia-plum hair dye and affix a safety pin to her earlobe, noting how she went to great pains to look decidedly unlike the fresh-faced preppies on my favorite sitcoms. At any given time, her musical allegiance fell to whoever most brought sense to her life, singing songs of truth that comforted purple-haired misfits across the nation. When she was stricken with a bout of teenage angst, I knew by the smoke wafting from underneath her door that I'd find her commiserating in front of her speakers, her bedroom darkened except for the faint red glow of the incense stick and whatever daylight dared sneak past her window shades. In contrast, a pulsating beat from her bedroom—which often prompted my mother to jab the kitchen ceiling with a broomstick—told me she was feeling unusually chipper. After the fall of Frampton, the words "gorgeous hair" never again passed her lips, and I promised myself never to get caught in the bubble-gum trap stocked with well-groomed preppy musicians—unless, of course, the preppies knew a thing or two about song hooks. Such pop detritus was for the musically ignorant, those who had been too unhip to recognize the difference between a manufactured boy band and an honest-to-goodness musical prodigy.

The music was the crux. It was all that mattered. And no amount of hairspray, lipstick, or unnecessary umlauts in a band name could compensate for a lack of innate musical savvy.

Marta was still waiting for my answer. Had the roles been reversed and she had been visiting my turf, I would probably have told her exactly what I thought of groupies and star-struck wannabes. But the scene was set, and pissing off my host was the last thing I wanted, particularly considering my valuables were being held hostage at her friend's house. Not being well versed in diplomacy, I shifted to a more submissive gear.

"I think Alan's hot." I could almost feel my dignity handing in a letter of resignation.

"Alan?" Marta contemplated my choice of band hottie. "Yeah, I can see that," she approved, although I couldn't have imagined her rebuking a crush on Martin or Fletch either. "You don't see him much in the videos, but he's not so bad."

I had, in fact, always found Alan Wilder to be the most physically—and, of course, artistically—alluring of the Depeche crew, and often fell asleep staring up at his image on the poster next to my bed—a few inches away from where Frampton had once hung, now that Janys had moved out and I'd taken over her more spacious room. But my crush only went so far. I never deigned to write "Jenna Rose Wilder" on my history binder or daydreamed romantic scenarios where Alan declared he'd sooner play disco than live without me. My most extravagant indulgence had been a crush on a guy who held a slight resemblance to the only classically trained member of the band.

After a while, once Marta had slid to the floor and put on her headphones, I began to stare out the back of the train.

It wasn't long before dawn approached, and I noticed immediately by the change of the gray forms outside that we had entered a different region. Instead of the flat red land I had come to believe comprised the whole of Spain, I saw a rolling, tree-filled wilderness. I still couldn't discern full details of the scenery, and the early-morning colors seemed like muted pastels that gradually claimed form and substance. Soon

I could see that we were riding on the edge of a ravine that dipped down to a river some one hundred feet below. All about the sides of the chasm stood craggy slopes flooded with greenery and tangles of foliage. The dawn turned the air pink and I felt relief when I hadn't even realized I'd been tense. It was as if the train had carried me through a dark land and delivered me into one of light, and my fears and desperations about the trip now all seemed absurd: All would be okay. I no longer felt like a lone traveler at the whim of my host. She and I were now traveling the same path, with the same fate awaiting us at the end. Although that fate was still unknown, it gave me comfort to think that, were it unpleasant, someone else would share the same misfortune. I now understood the allure of a traveling companion.

I began noticing figures running onto the tracks from behind the train. No sooner would our car pass than several scurrying gray masses would appear and bend over the rails. This happened sporadically, about every quarter mile or so. As the day slowly unfolded, the figures grew more distinct and no longer looked like large animals, as I had thought them to be, but people. Spaniards of all sizes and ages, about six or seven at a time, appeared from either side of the tracks as soon as the train had safely passed. Some slid down from hiding spots up on the cliff to the left, others climbed up from the ravine to the right. Then the train would snake away around a corner, carrying me off through the mountains and valleys and out of viewing distance of the peculiar activity before I could tell what they were doing. I looked over at Marta to ask but found her asleep, her head tilted to one side, the static from her headphones a slight hum.

I turned back to the window. Eventually the enigmatic rail-raiders stopped showing themselves and the train entered open country. We began to slow and, having forgotten the name of the town where we were headed, I woke Marta to ask if this was our stop. Her eyes opened wide and she brightened, the awareness of our arrival hitting her like the stale air from the bathroom. She peered outside at our new surroundings. Even after a night on a frigid train floor, the sight before her made all tension evaporate from her body. "Yes, this is my hometown. We've arrived."

4

After the darkness of the train compartment, the morning sun in Pontevedra burned my retinas so much that sunglasses were an imperative. The town, only a few minutes walk up a dusty road from the station, had just begun to wake when we breached the hill, which showed the city spread out before us. Pontevedra was situated on several hills and surrounded by lush green lands, with stores, homes, and other signs of suburbia flowing across the hilltops.

Marta had spent her formative years in León but still considered Pontevedra her home. Until we'd arrived in the coastal burg, I hadn't realized what hometown pride truly meant.

"This is my hometown," Marta told me, her voice alive and alert despite our sleepless train ride. "Depeche Mode is coming to my hometown. Do you know what that means for us here? Pontevedra is small"—her outstretched practically reached to either side of the city limits—"so when they announced that such a great band was coming here, everyone couldn't believe it." Her eyes widened to emphasize her surprise and her hand gestures became even more manic. "It was... like a dream. Depeche Mode? Here? In Pontevedra? It couldn't be." She gazed off as if watching angels alight on the coastline. Her reverence to the cathedral in León seemed like a marketing ploy compared to her earnest posturing atop the Pontevedra hills. "So now, we are here. And someplace in Pontevedra, so are they."

With those last words, my heart surged with more excitement than when I'd learned I was going to Disney World in sixth grade. The thought of my idols—the creators behind the music that influenced every decision in my life—residing in the same town, possibly only meters away, got my blood pumping so hot I could practically feel it pulsing through my veins.

But it was still nothing compared to Marta's emotions. Her words seemed obsessive, almost religious, as if the entire basis of her life depended on these four strangers. She stared down the road without looking at me, her eyes scanning the various storefronts and apartment buildings as if she sensed where one of them was gazing out a window or cutting their gums on a bocadillo.

"They are here and we will find them. We're staying in their hotel, you know."

I raised my eyebrows in surprise. "You know where they're staying?" I wasn't even certain she'd planned far enough ahead to ensure we didn't end up sleeping on park benches.

Marta stopped in her tracks and I, not knowing where to go without her leading, followed suit. In my less than forty-eight hours in Spain, I had already observed, much to the chagrin of my New York affinity for efficiency, that the majority of Spanish natives were incapable of walking and talking at the same time. And even though we had no place to go, and all the time in the world to get there, it irked me to stand stock still while Marta spoke.

"Look at the city, Zhane." She motioned out over the side of the hill, where a quaint seaside village lay spread before me. Few of the buildings were taller than ten stories, excepting the many obligatory church spires. "There are only two five-star hotels in all of Pontevedra—and they probably paid dearly for those ratings, although they of course more than deserved them." I allowed the statement to pass without comment. "That means there are only two places we need to look. But first, before we find the hotel, we must get our tickets from my cousin."

As Marta explained our agenda for the day, she stood rooted to the spot, while I, with not-so-subtle hints, tried to urge her onward into town. At that moment, the last thing I wanted was to wait for the sun to rise and roast my skin to a delicate rosy glow. I didn't know how far across town Marta's cousin lived, but I could tell we would be walking. From our short stint in Madrid, I had inferred that Marta had a clinical aversion to taxis, and I doubted Pontevedra had a subway or any other form of mass transit, other than possibly donkey train.

I wanted my hotel room. I wanted a nice warm bed with blankets and a soft mattress that I didn't have to share with some creepy vagabond or Eurail brat. I wanted peace and darkness and a nice long nap away from sunlight. I didn't want to stand in the middle of the street and get hit by a go-cart posing as a car while Marta explained our agenda.

"We must be careful because my parents do not know we are here. We cannot let my aunt see me or there will be big trouble." She widened her eyes. "*Big* trouble."

Since Marta had already confessed to being kicked out of her home, I couldn't imagine what difference it would make to be caught in another town. But then I considered what it would mean to get grounded by my parents (although that had yet to happen, ever) and then having them find out I'd gone to Miami for the weekend. I could see the predicament.

I tried a diplomatic approach. "Can we walk and talk at the same time? I'd like to catnap at some point."

Marta surveyed her hometown with hands on her hips, a Peter Pan-like figure. "Maybe we will see Depeche Mode in the lobby. Would you like that?" she asked as if offering me an ice cream cone.

Despite the heat, even ice cream had no appeal due to my fatigue. "Yes, but I think I'd appreciate them even more after a siesta."

"You sleep too much. I slept less than you and I'm not tired." There was no end to her competitiveness.

"That's because you stop and rest whenever you talk." I perched next to her, surveying her land with hands on hips to show I was her equal. "You conserve more energy than me."

She gazed out towards the coastline for a few minutes longer, almost as if she wanted to be certain the Moors weren't again attacking. Finally she took the hint and, much to my relief, continued walking.

* * *

We picked up our concert tickets from Marta's cousin on the far side of town, then trekked back up and down a few hills in search of the two hotels that might be housing our own personal holy grail. Marta inquired at the front desk of the first to see if the band was in fact staying there. She returned outside wearing a disappointed look.

"Do you think they'd actually tell you if they were staying there?" I asked. "I mean, couldn't they get fired for that?"

Marta shrugged. "I believe him. He was young. He would have

told us." She pointed to a hill we had already climbed several times over. "I think the other hotel is that way."

"It would have to be uphill, wouldn't it?" I mumbled.

"What did you say?"

"Nothing."

"Album six, track nine," Marta said without missing a beat. It took me a moment before I realized she was referring to a song title. Her quickness in such matters reminded me of a priest reciting scripture.

The next hotel lobby seemed rather plain for that of a five-star accommodation, and I began to wonder if the band was actually staying in the city proper when Marta grabbed my arm and squeezed it with the grip of a roadie on steroids. "Andy Franks. Look."

"Who?"

She nodded toward the man arguing with the woman behind the front desk. Although they were speaking English, it was clear that the hotel employee didn't understand everything that passed between them.

Marta glanced at me with a look of disbelief. "You do not know who Andy Franks is? And you call yourself a Moder? Aye aye aye!" She slapped her forehead with the heel of her hand. "Andy Franks is their *tour manager*. Didn't you see *101?*" I had seen the band documentary in question several dozen times. I just hadn't made Cliffs Notes. "Well, we know now that they are here."

It was then that I realized that the hotel was probably going to cost a little bit more than the Hotel Ríosol back in León. Marta strolled up to the desk, her eyes riveted on Andy Franks. We listened while he continued to argue with the woman—something about a breakfast buffet that he didn't want to pay for. Marta began talking rapidly in Spanish to the other desk clerk, then made it quite clear that she also spoke English by translating to me in a loud voice. "It will be 5,000 pesetas for the night." That wasn't too bad: about 100 dollars. My wallet could handle that. "A piece."

That was a little steep, but I went along with it, knowing full well that Marta would have it no other way. Besides, if she was willing to shell out the dough, I certainly wasn't going to be the one to keep us from sharing neighboring accommodations with our boys. By the time we had paid up at the front desk, Andy Franks had left. Marta, though slightly disappointed that she hadn't gotten the chance to hit him up for backstage passes, displayed a content smile as we took our hotel keys and rode the elevator to our room.

I claimed my bed by face-planting onto it. "I think I'll just pass out for a few days. Weeks, maybe."

While I snuggled down into the comforter, Marta continued strategizing. She could have benefited greatly from a large table map, Risk tokens, and a monocle. "We are in the same hotel as them, Zhane."

I turned a tired head toward her. A few hours earlier she had been downright giddy just being in the same town. I didn't know what to expect now that we were in the very building where they showered and slept. "I know, Marta. And as soon as I get a few hours rest, I'll be able to appreciate this more."

Marta hadn't stopped smiling since she had laid eyes on Andy Franks, and she left the room with the same ecstatic look on her face. "I'm going to go look. Maybe they are even *on this floor*."

* * *

"Zhane! Zhane! Wake up! Listen, listen."

I rolled over in my bed, luxuriating in horizontal sleep. "Marta, I was—"

"Shh! Listen!"

I shut my mouth and did as Marta ordered, not knowing what I was listening for but listening all the same. Then, I heard it. It was singing.

"Do you think that is one of them?" Marta asked, her head tilted heavenwards as if listening for an angelic choir. "Which one do you think it is? Zhane, you speak English. Get dressed! Go in the hall! Look!"

In my half-conscious state, I leapt up from my bed and found my shorts, which were lying on the floor. My body, not yet fully awake and coordinated, allowed me to trip several times before successfully pulling them on. I took a quick peek in the mirror, Marta rushing me the entire time, then, still buttoning my shorts, stepped out of our room in time to see a door at the direct opposite end of the hall slam shut.

I returned to our room to a bombardment of questions. "I don't know. I don't *know*. I didn't see anyone. The door closed as soon as I went out there."

Marta sat down on the bed analyzing the event. "Who did it sound like to you? Did he sound British?"

To me, all voices had the same accentless accent when singing, but there was something about this one that was remotely familiar. I turned the question on her. "Who do you think it was?"

Marta concentrated her gaze. "Martin."

I had been hesitant to admit it, but I thought I'd seen a floppy blond head at the end of the hall. "Me too." I crawled back between the sheets, my heart beating a little faster than before.

Marta fell backwards on the bed, her arms to her sides. "This... this is heaven!"

* * *

"Zhane, time to get up." I blinked my eyes in the grayness of the hotel room and glanced at my watch. It was only three in the afternoon. "Come on. Let's go."

"What? What do you mean?" I curled further under the covers as Marta opened wide the curtains that gave us a grand view of a Pontevedra alley. I raised an arm to shield myself from the sun. "Come on, Marta. We've got nearly five hours."

"Uh-uh. Let's go. We have to get on line."

My face remained buried in my pillow. "I thought we already had our tickets. Isn't that what we picked up from your cousin yesterday?"

"Yes, yes. But if we want to have good seats, we should be standing in line *now*. "

I sat up on the bed, my eyes still unable to focus. "Now? You mean they're general admission?" I'd heard Europe was behind the times and was perhaps a tad technologically challenged, but the thought of general-admission tickets seemed preposterous. What next? Wearing togas to the amphitheater?

Marta looked perplexed and, for once, impatient, as if an explanation would waste precious time.

"Aren't there any assigned seats?" I asked, but the puzzlement remained on her face. "How do we know where to sit? Is it like some big Woodstock thing or something?"

"Woodstock? No, this isn't some American hippie festival." Marta gazed at me as if such an Americanism had caused tumors to spontaneously form on her frontal lobe. "But we do not have assigned seats, which means we have to get there early. It would be nice to have front row, no?"

Front row? There was actually the possibility that I could have front-row seats to a concert without having to give a scalper a kidney? I was out of bed and dressed before Marta could say *puta madre*.

We walked through Pontevedra, Marta pointing out the interesting sites from her childhood, the pride ringing clearly in her voice. "We will come back here next week with my parents for some Celtic celebrations." She described the festivities that sounded at once debaucherous and charming. "And when we do, you were never here."

I picked up on the hint. "Pontevedra? What's Pontevedra?"

Marta smiled. "Good. You are a fast learner." She looked me up and down rather quickly. "We will have to take you shopping. You still wear this big 'Made in America' sign on your forehead." She smiled, although I knew her words were not meant as a compliment.

I gave Marta a once-over and considered what a shopping spree in a Spanish department store would get me. "Marta, seriously, if I bought clothes here, do you really think I'd look Spanish?" I twirled a piece of my red hair, which was becoming even brighter with each day under the Spanish sun. I had considered dying it black before going to Europe, just for a change, but that was after I had already sent Marta my description of what to look for in the airport and I'd been afraid she wouldn't have recognized me.

"No, you are right. You'd look like a chipper."

"Uh. *¿Que?*"

"A chipper." She stopped in her tracks, as was her custom. "I think maybe it is English slang. *British* English. I learned a lot of it when I was in London. My friends in London told me that a chipper is someone who tries to be something they are not. And they look bad doing it."

I nodded my head. "A poseur. That's what we call them in the U.S."

"Poseur? I will remember that." She resumed walking. "Yes, you would look like a Spanish chipper—*poseur*—with different clothes. Not just because of your hair either. You're very tall and your skin is too white. You need more sun. By the time you leave Spain though, that will be done. People will *know* you've been to Spain."

"I think I've had more sun in the past few days than I got all last summer. I'm surprised I haven't burned yet. I fry. Crispy fry."

Marta, although she had been correct about many of her predictions for my Spanish visit, could not have been more wrong about her forecast for my sun exposure. The next twenty-four hours were about to reshape the rest of my Spanish vacation.

After about a mile or so, we reached Estadio Pasarón, where twenty or so other people already waited in line. We sat and prepared to wait it out, sheltered from the orange heat by the shade of the arena wall. Even Marta seemed disturbed by the temperature. She became a twinge irritable and declared that day "Tuesday the 13th" due to the Train Ride From Hell and the sweltering weather.

Although we soon stopped our complaining, we didn't feel any better. The topic of conversation turned to why I changed my address so often.

"Well, I grew up on Long Island—that's where West Hempstead is. I go to school in Michigan, and I lived in Manhattan over the summer. So I've only changed my address *completely* twice. It's just that every once in a while, I change back to one of the old ones, depending on what time of year it is."

"And you go to school in Michigan? Why Michigan?"

I had discovered that Europeans, if you try to tell them the geography of your country without their having asked first, will become insulted that you think them uneducated. So I didn't begin by explaining where Michigan was, as was my first instinct, but by explaining why I wasn't at UCLA, my dream school since the time I was old enough to plan for a life beyond parental frontiers.

"Michigan is not a bad place, don't get me wrong. It's just that it's so *cold*."

Marta stared up at the hazy sky. "I could take a little cold right now."

"Uh-uh, give me blazing heat over frostbite any day." I poked my snow-white skin to test for reddening. "Now, if you picked up Ann Arbor and placed it on Venice Beach, it'd be perfect. Academically, Michigan's a great school, but it's in the middle of *nowhere*. After living in the biggest and best—" I caught myself, knowing that Marta would challenge such a statement. I wasn't up to a round of Madrid vs. New York posturing, even though I didn't even consider it a fair fight. "...*One* of the best cities in the world, Ann Arbor is downright, well, *tame*. Borderline boring. But at least it's a big school, which is why I finally chose it over the others I applied to. Trust me, I didn't choose it for the location. Nobody's from Michigan. I'm probably the only person you'll ever meet who's been there, let alone *lived* there."

After what seemed like an eternity, our mouths parched even after several trips to the soda vendor conveniently situated just across the alley, the admission process began. About a hundred people were lined up by this time, and Marta and I pressed our way closer to the front. Marta kept urging me further ahead: "Push them, Zhane! You're an American! Be rude!"

Once in, I took off, my eyes set on my goal of the stage ahead of me. About halfway across the field, I turned and noticed Marta some distance behind. She waved me on, "Go! Save me a place!" I kept running. I thought how glad Marta must have been that I was a "tall

American." Although I'd never been known for speed—my softball coach always put in a pinch runner if I made it on base—my legs took me faster than everyone around me. Out of breath, I staked our claim a little to stage right. Front row.

FRONT FUCKING ROW.

The reality hit me just as I was recovering my breath. Never in my life had I been so close, let alone *front fucking row.* My father had shelled out some hefty kale (or forgiven a few debts) for my Giants Stadium seats, and even those had been at least a hundred yards from the stage. *Front fucking row.* I hadn't even believed it possible. Perhaps it hadn't been my long legs. Perhaps if my coach had dangled front-row tickets over first base I would have made it to the bag. Screw the pinch runner.

Marta showed up moments later, looking in worse physical shape than I was. "Front row! We have front row!" she panted, patting my shoulder as if rewarding an obedient dog.

I slid down against the crowd-control barricade in front of the stage, which offered some refuge from the sun but was more than a little uncomfortable due to the iron grating we were forced to sit on. The waffle-like indentations on my bare legs, however, were worth it. "Still think this is Tuesday the 13th?" I asked. Marta flashed the most dazzling smile I'd seen on her yet. She didn't even need to answer.

After going on a spending spree at the merchandise booth, Marta returned to the FFR with a long-sleeved tee, a necklace, and several other trinkets. I, realizing we would be going to more concerts, decided to wait to buy my souvenirs.

She stared at her necklace, a piece of metal with holes punched out on the end of a long black cord. "Ah, I think this is Martin."

"What do you mean?" I inspected the abstract design, which could have been a Rorschach test for all I knew. "Looks like two holes to me."

"Yes. It is Martin. Look at my shirt. It is him."

I surveyed her newly acquired clothing, knowing I'd see her in this garb quite often over the next few days. The shirt had four sets of blotches, two blotches apiece, one set on each arm and front or back of the shirt. In the bottom corner of each set were numbers. "These are Depeche Mode," she said, pointing to the blotches. "I think that is Martin. Ah, look! Yes, it is."

I didn't care *who* was on the necklace. I didn't even think the irregularly cut holes were meant to be anything other than decorative. But I wanted to know what made Marta think they were the band members.

"Look, these numbers. They are their birthdays. You do not know their birthdays?" She looked both shocked and appalled. I nearly laughed.

"Well, not off the top of my head, no." I had taken to overusing idioms in an attempt to test her language skills, at which point she'd have to ask what I meant and allow me to change the subject. This time it worked because something more important came to her mind.

"Now, you have your membership card?" By this, she meant my Depeche Mode Bong Fan Club card. Before I'd even left the states, Marta had reminded me of this most important of documents several times over, leading me to believe it would be more useful than even my passport. There was no possible way I could have forgotten it.

"Yes. In my back pocket. Don't leave home without it, right?"

Marta had this strange notion that, because I was an American and possessed this obviously vital piece of laminated plastic, I could ask the security guards for backstage passes and they would kowtow as they handed them over to me. I decided it couldn't hurt to pack it.

As I rested my head against the crowd barrier, my tireless companion began to complain about a girl named Adrienne who was supposed to have bought concert tickets for the French venues but had backed out at the last minute. Crude words directed at this French girl rolled off her lips every few seconds, some of which I didn't understand and assumed were British. "You know I love languages, Zhane. I've taken English, Russian, and German, and next semester I will take Japanese. I don't like France. I don't like French people. I don't like the French language. But I had written to Adrienne for a while and I thought that maybe she was different." She threw her hands up into the air. "Of course not. She is *French*. She probably got tickets for the Spanish venues some other way and so she didn't need me." She slapped her hand twice against her cheek, a gesture I had come to understand as sarcastic for "poor thing" or a sign that someone is spoiled. "She is probably here someplace. And if I see her..." She scouted the immediate area, perhaps for a girl with *Made in France* written on her forehead.

A breeze had picked up and the sun had almost ducked below the side of the arena. It was after nine, but we guessed that they were probably waiting for complete darkness for the ultimate effect. The anxious crowd began to stand and chant a melody that Marta referred to as the "football chorus." Because it lacked words, I caught on easily and joined in with the rest of the population so that, for the moment at least, I felt somewhat like a Spaniard.

But that tune didn't last very long and soon they began another one—with lyrics—that sounded as if I had heard it before, perhaps on *Bugs Bunny.* "We are complaining," Marta explained the second time the chorus of *"Aye, aye, aye, aye"* began. I decided I liked a country that had a nationally known song based on the concept of complaining.

The arena was scarcely filled by the time the lights came up and the opening band took the stage. I scanned the paltry number of people and wondered if this were typical of a European concert. "When we go to Madrid, it will be much different," Marta assured me.

The opening act was an Irish rap group called Marxman. Upon hearing this description, I expected to be less than thrilled with the music but instead was pleasantly surprised. In any case, I figured I'd better get used to them. There were several other concerts ahead of me that they'd be opening for.

Marta, on the other hand, was far from pleased, and from her perspective, I could hardly blame her. One song had a chorus of "Fuck Columbus," and the frontman tried to get the Spanish audience to join in. I myself found the gesture in poor taste and thought it rather asinine of them to play such a song in Spain, let alone coax the audience into deriding a national hero. Though the theme of the song wasn't really directed at Columbus himself, but more at the destruction he brought to the New World, most of the crowd probably didn't understand any more than those two words. I even had trouble making out what was said since the lead singer practically ate the mic as he rapped.

Their set done, Marxman left the stage and the crew clambered on, making scenery changes and last-minute adjustments. I leaned against the barrier next to Marta, my rear now sore and completely waffled from the crowd-control barrier. We could do little more than face forward because of the crowd pressing up behind us, but after a while, they ceased to exist. Only the stage before me mattered. I watched in envy as the crew scrambled up and through the riggings, dangling precariously several stories above the heads of the audience without a rope. They hoisted large curtains over the front of the stage and pushed off the old instruments while dragging on new ones. I could feel Marta growing tense with excitement.

"There!" Marta grabbed my upper arm and twisted me in the direction of one of the bodyguards. "Get your card out and talk to him!" I didn't need further edification as to which card she meant. This was one of the few situations where Dad's Amex wasn't going to get me anywhere.

I tried to discern who among the mob of roadies and security guards she was referring to. "*Him!*" she said, irritated by my inherent stupidity. "The security man."

I took my card out of my back pocket and tried to hand it to her. "You do it. I don't speak Spanish."

She shoved my hand away. "He's *American*, Zhane."

I looked at the blond security guard, who, like myself, appeared to be relieved that the sun was finally setting. His head tilted backward as if comforted by the slight drop in temperature. "How do you know he's not British like the band?"

Marta rolled her eyes. "Can't you see the sign on his forehead? It's just like yours." I was reminded of our initial conversation at the airport, wherein I'd learned that a bright neon billboard proclaiming my nationality followed me wherever I went. Her words were accompanied by appropriate and frantic gestures—writing across her forehead, slapping me in my mine—one of the first times I'd actually witnessed her move faster than melting flan.

I decided it couldn't hurt to play the American-compatriot card and leaned over the barrier to try to get the guard's attention. I couldn't tell if he could see me, what with his extra-large, uber-dark shades—which, I concede, were terribly un-Euro—but after I flailed my arms a few minutes longer, I saw him leave his perch and walk over. It was then I realized that I didn't know what I was asking him about.

"What do I say?" I muttered to Marta as he strode over. "Why am I bothering him? He's working."

Her look told me she could only barely tolerate such stupidity. "You're from the American fan club and you want backstage passes. Go!" She shoved me towards him, despite the fact the crowd-control barrier wouldn't let me move a nanometer further.

I turned to find the security guard gazing down at me, probably amused by my exchange with Marta, who had turned away pretending to be oblivious of her surroundings. "Yeah, hi. I'm sorry to bother you—"

"No worries, I was practically falling asleep over there. This heat almost put me to sleep." He looked to be about forty, with skin that had seen its share of the sun and the requisite bodyguard muscles threatening to split his shirtsleeves. As Marta had predicted, his accent was definitively American. I'd hoped he'd at least be Australian so that, for once, Marta couldn't gloat about his forehead sign.

"Yeah, hot. Whew!" I fanned myself as if he spoke a different language and didn't understand the concept. I wasn't used to begging favors. "It gets hot in New York, but not like this."

"An American? What are you doing in this crowd?"

I flashed my Bong card. "I'm from the American fan club. I came all this way just to see them." By this time, our conversation had attracted the interest of several Spanish fans, who now turned to eavesdrop on what few English words they could recognize.

"New Yorker, huh?" He gave me a once-over. I couldn't tell if he was trying to peg what borough I was from or how big my cup size was. If it were the latter, I'm sure Marta would have offered up my services without hesitation. "I'm from Detroit. The whole of security is based there."

"Detroit?" I sensed Marta turning around. Things were going too well for her to butt in. "I go to school in Ann Arbor."

"You're a Wolverine? Small world." I saw him reach into the back of his ultra-tight jeans. "How's about I give a fellow Michigander a backstage pass?"

I almost fainted. I hadn't even had to ask. "You serious? I'd love one!" I felt an elbow enter my ribcage. "Actually, would it be okay if I had two? I'm with my Spanish friend." I made a motion towards Marta, who had remained uncharacteristically silent throughout the whole exchange.

The bodyguard smirked and handed me a second key to the kingdom. "Sure. No problem." After thanking him profusely, I introduced myself formally, then proceeded to gush my thanks some more. Bryan, as we learned he was called, enjoyed the reaction he'd incited and chuckled at my enthusiasm. "I'll see you backstage after the show." Over the top of his sunglasses his eyebrows twitched a goodbye before he returned to his sentry position in front of the stage.

I stared down at the two blue passes in my hands, barely able to comprehend how easy it had been. Marta snatched them from my grip just as a hand reached between us from behind. A cautionary slap kept any other fingers from attempting pilferage.

"Be careful, Zhane!" She shoved them down the front of her shirt. "These are more precious than gold. Anyone around us might take them at any time." She shook her head as if I were a naughty child.

For the first time since I'd arrived in Spain, I felt my body brimming with anger. I'd put up with quite a bit so far and had, uncharacteristically for me, said nothing out of fear of upsetting the one person I knew in this foreign land. Back home, no one who knew me would have dared snatch a stick of gum from my hand, let alone prized backstage passes.

I held out my hand and glared at Marta.

"What?" One eyebrow bent upwards to indicate her confusion.

"My pass, Marta." I kept my eyes locked with hers, my voice low and steady in a tone I saved for special occasions that required a smidge of intimidation. "Now."

With a movement even slower than usual, Marta reached down the front of her shirt as if being asked to relinquish a vital organ. Neither of us dropped our gaze as she returned one pass to me. I made a point of wiping her sweat off on my shorts before removing the adhesive and slapping it proudly above my left breast. Marta turned back to face the stage, her eyes deliberately avoiding me for the next several minutes.

With the sun having already set at a little after 10PM, a cool breeze had picked up and the curtains whipped about uncontrollably. The audience commenced with their Complaining Song, this time with more conviction. Eventually the crew took down the curtains and the spotlight technicians took their places in the rigging, a sure sign the performance was mere moments away.

The crowd erupted when the arena's house lights finally dimmed. I felt the air rush from my lungs as the thousands of fans behind shoved us against the railing in an attempt to get a few inches closer. When a particularly rambunctious chipper began flailing her arms around Marta's body, she was rewarded with a quick elbow to the gut. I expected a fight to break out, but one look from Marta put the chipper in her place.

"She learns quickly," Marta smirked.

The screaming became so loud that it was soon reduced to a ringing in my ears as four very recognizable silhouettes took to the stage, three on raised platforms with their respective instruments. A full bar of music hadn't played when Marta and I turned to each other and, in a single conspiratorial shriek, exclaimed, "'Higher Love'!" It wouldn't have mattered what song they'd chosen to open with, our reaction would have been the same. What mattered was seeing them in the flesh, communing with thousands of other like-minded souls, and, of course, having the front row. That alone cemented our status as Most Devoted. For that show, at least.

"Look at him, Zhane," Marta sighed in my ear as lead singer Dave Gahan strutted about the stage, his once clean-cut looks now transformed into post-grunge scruff. "He is the most wonderful, sexy man I could ever imagine. In fact, he is—" I covered my ears as she let out a piercing shriek.

Dave was standing directly in front of us, thrusting his hips in a trademark move that would have made Elvis blush. Marta gripped my arm so tightly my fingers tingled from lack of circulation. "I think I may pass out." She fanned her other hand in front of her face, alternately screaming and sighing as if suffering from lack of oxygen. When Dave strutted to the far end of the stage, she regained her composure. "He is the ultimate rock god." She turned her green-eyed gaze to me. "Alan looks hot tonight, no?"

I glanced stage left at Alan, who was ensconced behind a drum set. After lead singers and bass players, drummers are the most sought-after band member, often trailing behind harmonica players and accordionists, perhaps due to their inconspicuous location behind mounds of equipment. This being Depeche's first drum-enhanced outing—previous efforts and supporting tours were purely electronic—Alan had the benefit of displaying his percussive prowess up front, not relegated to the back of the stage, as in most bands. I remembered reading an article about how, in their early days, the band would place the drum machine smack dab in the middle of the stage, lest they stood accused of hiding their reliance on electronics. Now Alan, although not front and center, proved his musical dexterity once again with his newly acquired drum skills. And I was smitten.

Four songs into the set, I found myself getting caught up in Marta's DM love fest, and the two of us began swapping sexual allusions about Dave and Alan. We had just the combination of naivety and sexual curiosity to sound absolutely ludicrous to those around us, but because we spoke in English, Marta assured me our banter would remain confidential to those around us. "Look at those hips," she murmured, her throaty voice providing the perfect cadence to her indecency. "What I wouldn't do..." She kept Dave in her gaze as he gyrated some more, squinting her eyes to line up her target and squeezing hands.

The band was in the midst of "Behind the Wheel," the innuendo-laden single from 1987's *Music for the Masses*, and Marta used her front-row position to catch Dave's attention. I nearly fainted when he crossed the stage, squatted down to better look us in the eye, and—for four ecstatic lines—sang straight to her. Marta's enthusiasm—personified with emphatic hand gestures and top-of-her-lungs vocals—shone so much that Dave stood up and pointed her out to the rest of the audience, an example for the rest of his admirers to follow. When finally he strutted away to croon to some other starry-eyed female, Marta stumbled against my shoulder. Had we not been crammed up against the crowd-control barrier, she might have fainted straight to the ground.

"That was better than sex," she managed, her voice a thin thread of raspy gratification. "If I got the chance, I'd go right up to that man and… and…" Marta stared at Dave, who was now twirling frantically with the mic stand, another one of his trademark maneuvers. She sighed as he came out of his spin and raised the stand over his head in triumph before pumping the air once with his crotch.

"Gross," I said, almost under my breath. But Marta heard me.

"If that were Alan, you wouldn't be saying that." I glanced over as "my man," as Marta soon dubbed him, worked frantically through "I Feel You," off *Songs of Faith and Devotion* (or *SOFAD,* as their latest album was often abbreviated). Behind him, on the large screens that displayed the projections (seen only at live performances), shone the silhouettes of each of the band members performing their respective duties: Martin strumming the hypnotic guitar hook, Alan pounding the skins, Dave making Marta's dreaded Jesus postures, and Fletch incongruously raising his fists as if pumping iron, further proof that his managerial responsibilities were eclipsing his musical roles. When the lights hit just right, I could see the beads of sweat fly off Alan's face and land on the fans in the front row. By playing the role of lust-happy groupie, I was slowly becoming one, and I vowed that during my next pre-concert seat-staking sprint, I would aim for stage left.

At the end of "Never Let Me Down Again," when the crowd began the obligatory arm-waving that had become de rigueur for performances ever since it was documented in *101,* I glanced around me, hardly able to believe what I was experiencing. I was in Spain under a starry, cloudless sky, mere feet from my idols, a backstage pass slapped above my left breast. Around me an arena of fans waved their arms in unison, like sea grass swayed by the tide. As the stage lights shone over my face, alternating between the blues and reds that Anton Corbijn—the director/photographer responsible for the band's trademark visuals—had incorporated into the band's performances,

I felt as if I finally experienced my own version of a religious ecstasy, complete with swooning believers among the congregation.

When the band left the stage for the first encore, a bittersweet pang hit my chest. The concert would be ending soon, and I could feel the euphoria begin to wane. Then I remembered our backstage passes. Marta and I, the tension of the pass-snatching now behind us, began anticipating what the encores would be, our voices volleying back and forth over the roar of the crowd's Complaining Song. With each guess, we'd present numerous reasons for and against each song, our debate becoming as serious as a courtroom drama. "They will *not* play 'Just Can't Get Enough.' That's too much a Vince song." "Of *course* they'll play 'Everything Counts.' That will be the final song. I am certain." "I wish they'd play 'Stories of Old.' They've *never* played that live. *Ever.*"

"Do you think they will play 'Fly on the Windscreen'?" As I started to shake my head, I realized I had once again fallen into Marta's trap of questioning. She wasn't really asking me. "Of course they will. It is a concert staple. Chin up—it's not 'Stories of Old,' but you will love this, too."

While they, of course, didn't play a single one of the obscure favorites I'd hoped for, they did hit the biggies: "Enjoy the Silence," "Personal Jesus," and, as Marta had predicted, "Fly on the Windscreen." Within the first two notes, a smug grin had spread across her face and she nodded her head to the beat as if they had been awaiting her approval. Then, before I had a chance to protect my ears, Marta emitted a shriek that left my eyeballs quivering. Dave's prancing had brought him back to our side of the stage, and Marta once again attempted to capture his attention, but to no avail. Her bearded Romeo chose another devotee to sing to this time. I saw the smile slide off her face as Marta watched the buxom fan squeeze her cleavage in Dave's direction.

"She doesn't even know the words!" Marta declared as she watched the girl's miserable attempt to lip-synch the words to one of the band's most popular songs. "How *could* he? How could he pick such a chipper?" The concert nearly over, she was anxious at her final moments with her fantasy boyfriend.

I nudged her to get her attention as I began making hand gestures to the words. "Come here"—I beckoned—"Kiss me"—fingertips to my lips—"Now"—pointing to my chest. The corner of Marta's mouth twitched as she observed my idiotic behavior, but soon she was doing the same, and the two of us set our sights on getting Dave's attention. When he pranced back our way, he caught a glimpse of the two imbeciles in the front row performing their mime. Apparently this is more entertaining than it sounds, as Dave squatted in front of us and watched our moronic shtick for a few choruses. He then stood, pointed down at us, and—our hearts almost stopped and fell out of our chests—*began mimicking us.*

Before Marta and I knew what was happening, the rest of the crowd was acting as spastic as we were, pantomiming our actions in unison. When I turned around, I witnessed the whole of the arena copying our hair-brained routine. After the initial shock, I felt a warm glow of satisfaction: My idiocy had unwittingly impacted Depeche history.

Nothing could have given me greater elation. Only rock stars held such influence, the power to control an entire stadium and have the crowd do one's bidding. But there I was, a front-row spectator, somehow manipulating the crowd via my onstage avatar. There has never been a time, before or since, that I more greatly regretted having quit the drums in eighth grade, thereby negating all hope of rock stardom.

My head spun with visions of future concerts and other, larger arenas brimming with fans performing my pantomime. I'd have to wait for two days to see if Dave incorporated it into his act in Madrid.

One more song and the set had ended, leaving Marta and me breathless at the railing, as if we had just given a performance ourselves. I watched her eyes twinkle as she reached into her shirt and slapped her pass on her chest. "Ready for the next adventure, Zhane?"

5

The crowd around us began to thin, and Marta and I watched as the majority headed towards the exit, while a select assortment of fans of a particular nature headed straight towards the front of the stage, where security was allowing entry only to the privileged. We watched as several teary-eyed faces were turned away, and as they passed by, I lay a protective hand over my backstage sticker.

"Go on, Zhane. I'll follow." I was amazed at how quickly Marta assumed a submissive role, especially considering the circumstances. Alone with me, she was pure confidence, often to a fault. But once amid a crowd of English-speakers, she deferred to my native skills. Considering how competent her English was, I didn't understand the flagging self-confidence.

As Marta switched gears and fell in behind me, I led the way to the front of the line. Our old friend Bryan was letting people in and greeted me by name. Without even looking at her, I could sense

Marta puff with pride as we were admitted to the Promised Land. As I shook Bryan's hand, I spotted the chipper who had been behind us the whole concert. She stood among those denied backstage access and, when she spotted me and Marta, she spat what I took to be an insult. Marta spun on her heels and began barking a barrage of insults so fierce that I had to pull her back by the collar.

"Marta! Don't, just let it go." She pulled like a pit bull on a leash. "Come on, you don't want to get us kicked out, do you?" That seemed to calm her. A moment later, she'd regained her composure and was in step behind me. We ducked into a bathroom for a last-minute makeup and hair check then, properly preened, strode into the main event.

I'd had dreams of what backstage would be like. There'd be a huge party, a veritable nightclub full of celebs and their closest friends, with a few nameless VIPs thrown in for good measure. Champagne would flow from a fountain, and we'd all mingle and laugh as we exchanged bons mots. Every once in a while, I'd be interrupted and asked to pose for a photo for the society pages. This, of course, was before we took off for the true party at a nightclub or hotel penthouse where we'd get plastered and commit acts that would make Mick Jagger blush.

As with most preconceived notions of the glamorous life, I was mistaken about the reality of backstage. We were led to a bare-bones room, only slightly bigger than my living room back on Long Island. On a folding table sat row upon row of bottled Spanish beer, while nearby stood an unmanned foosball table and high-backed armchair that would have been more at home in a tea parlor. A few nondescript roadies congregated to knock back post-show brews, while small clusters of lucky fans such as ourselves huddled nervously together.

After my initial disappointment at the decided lack of glamour, I focused on one particular object. "Foosball! Marta, you know how to play?"

She stared at me as if I'd just told her that Spain had been sold to France. "You are *not* serious."

"What's wrong?" There was a deathly stillness hanging over the backstage area that I knew could be eradicated with the cheerful patter of foosball goals.

Green eyes rolled like marbles. "Forget it, Zhane. Let's just get some beer."

After grabbing our *cervezas*, much appreciated after hours of sweating in the hot evening air, we joined the ranks of the wallflowers along the perimeter, scanning the room every few moments for a glimpse of anyone who even remotely resembled a band member.

"There she is," Marta murmured, motioning towards a petite blonde girl on the other side of the room. "It's her, the frog." I'd only recently learned this as a nickname for French people and didn't expect Marta to know the slang. Then again, her aversion to the French was almost as great as the pride in her country, so she may have coined half the derogatory terms herself. "It's Adrienne. I'm going to say something to her."

I held out an arm to restrain her. "Marta, we're backstage. *Backstage.* Do you want to make a scene and get us kicked out?" I had a brief flicker of a fantasy, wherein Marta was escorted out and I was left with all four band members to myself. They gathered around me, raising their glasses in toast to my presence and hung on my every word. The vision vanished when I imagined Marta's jealous retaliation, which could include anything from locking me out of the hotel to telling Julio to toss my possessions in the León river. The blonde, spotting Marta's leer, averted her gaze and turned her back to us.

My traveling companion calmed but remained on high alert for any sign of a band member. After another ten minutes, her foot began to beat an impatient rhythm on the cement floor.

"They're not coming," Marta muttered, having long since forgotten my abandonment at the Madrid airport. "I knew it was too good to be true. Today is indeed Tuesday the 13th."

The words were hardly out of her mouth when I spotted Martin and Fletch. I nudged her with my elbow. "They're here." Marta's mouth snapped shut. "Look." Alan had joined the group. We stood rooted to the spot as surely as the statue of King Felipe III in the Plaza Mayor.

Marta's lips barely moved as she asked the question I'd been anticipating. "Where's Dave?"

"Dunno." The only movement I made was to raise the beer to my lips.

"Think he'll come? He must come. He *has* to."

"Dunno." I watched as Fletch settled himself into the armchair with a most unlikely rock star beverage, a cup of tea. "Is he serious?" I asked Marta, as if she held the answers to such questions. "Tea? Seriously?" I sniggered at the absurdity of the situation, which put me more at ease. "Want another beer?" Marta shook her head. "Hell, they're free."

The path to the beer table crossed right in front of Fletch, and I could feel the liquid courage I'd imbibed urging me towards him. "Awesome show tonight," I offered.

He finished a sip of tea. "Thanks. You a Yank?"

I nodded, unable to believe I was involved in idle chitchat with Andy Fletcher. I tried to think of something very un-fanlike to ask, something beyond the usual "What's your favorite album?" or "Which song do you just, like, *hate* playing live?"

"Do you mind all these people around you?" Marta had come up behind me, having found the courage to breach the linguistic barrier with someone other than me. "Wouldn't you prefer to wind down after a performance?"

Fletch seemed as amused by the question as by our tag-team interrogation. "Not at all. Being surrounded by women is ideal." I hadn't expected such a frank answer and nearly snorted beer out of my nose.

"Brilliant show. Really." Marta's words drew Fletch's attention from my social blunder. We waved at him and walked over to the beer table, where I steadied myself.

"Oh, dear Lord. We just spoke with Andy Fletcher." I popped open another beer and guzzled half of it in a single swig. Marta stared at me as if I'd just committed yet another faux-pas.

"You're like a real-life American college film." I was surprised at the lack of derision in her voice. In fact, for once she seemed somewhat awestruck, not simply at my capacity for drink—of which she'd seen little—but at the ease with which I'd approached Fletch.

I clinked my bottle against hers. "Under the circumstances, I'll take that as a compliment." I pointed towards Martin, who was swarming with girls, a wide, wonky grin spread across his face. "He ain't complaining."

Marta rubbed her lips as if contemplating something devious. "I'm going to get his autograph," she said decidedly. She handed me her beer. "Here, hold this."

A beer in each hand, I watched Marta slip easily past the chippers orbiting around the songwriter, worming her way into the nucleus. Her unflagging determination never ceased to amaze me.

"Thirsty?"

I turned to find myself inches away from Alan. I hadn't even heard him approach and, staring up at him, I realized I'd been severely mistaken in tenth grade, when I dated a pencil-necked geek who I thought bore a slight resemblance to this god of synth. There was no resemblance, could be no resemblance. The two weren't even of the same species. Their only similarity was dark hair and, on the geek's part, a passing attempt at musicianship.

I was not—and am not still—often dumbstruck by the beauty of someone of the opposite sex. Problems speaking in front of large crowds? Sometimes. Difficulty with tedious small talk? Heck, yeah. Gelatinized knees caused by the piercing gaze of a chiseled face, wavy hair, and a devilish grin? I can count the instances on a single hand—and three of those instances were with this same man.

As I mentioned before, I had not considered myself part of the Alan-worshipping camp when I boarded the plane to Madrid. I all but loathed shrieky groupies who pulled at their hair at the mere sight of their object of lust. It was degrading, repugnant, an aberrance of nature to behave in such a way. As with gods and geeks, there was a scientifically proven distinction between fans and fanatics. I considered myself part of the more evolved of the two, but I began to question my genetic composition as I attempted to answer his very simple one-word question.

"A… bit." I took a sip of beer, as if to prove the sincerity of my statement. The cool liquid seemed to muster confidence from the corners of my body where it was hiding. It was only then that I realized he was probably commenting on my double-fisted drinking. "Actually, just holding a friend's. She's over there." I started to point towards Marta, but she was busy body-checking a four-foot chipper, so I quickly drew Alan's attention back to me. "So, yeah, awesome show."

For the weeks leading up to my trip, I'd made multi-paged lists of intelligent-sounding questions that I would ask my idols, should I be fortunate enough to meet them in person. I'd categorized them, vetted them with my other Moder friends, everything short of indexing them. Not a single one of those questions came to mind at that moment.

"Glad you enjoyed it." His grin paralyzed me. In times of nervousness, I often relied upon brushing back my hair or twisting an earring to relieve the tension. With my hands full of beer, I only succeeded in knocking my chin with the bottle. "Have I met you before?"

I nearly laughed out loud. Met? *Me?* "No, we haven't," I said, grinning like an idiot at the mere thought. I suddenly wished I had a third leg to kick myself in the ass. I'd been given the perfect opportunity and had promptly flushed it. "Actually, once, but very briefly, back in New York."

I could pull this off. A few years earlier, a friend of mine had won tickets to the premiere of *101* and had offered me one—if I could get us a ride into the city. I'd begged my mother for a lift, but, as it was a school night, she didn't want to make the trek. Even when I told her it wasn't about seeing the movie but *meeting the band,* she scoffed, saying that wasn't important, and left me dragging my tail between my legs to relay the band news to Alejandro. When I saw him at school the next day, he pulled out photos of him and Alan. I cried all through chemistry and eventually skipped the rest of my classes to pout on a jetty at Jones Beach.

I recalled this moment and realized that Alan would have no recollection of the incident, and that I could very well pretend that I had been there and had a perfectly delightful conversation with him. "It was at the New York premiere of *101*. What was that, four years ago?"

He smirked, and I couldn't tell if it was because his bullshit detector had gone off or if he could hear the tremor in my voice. "Yeah, about that." He raised his rocks glass, which contained a cloudy concoction on ice, in salute. "To meeting again." I raised both beer bottles, realized what a drunken American ass I looked like, and clinked one against his. I credit the look in his eyes at that moment to making me consider a conversion to the dark side of groupiedom, or at least enjoying a momentary transgression.

"And again." I raised the other beer. I had managed two words more than I thought I had in me.

"All right. See you around." The god of synth raised his glass once more, then turned. I watched him vanish into a sea of giggling girls who reached out to touch various parts of his six-foot, leather-clad body as he passed.

I felt someone grip my arm. "You spoke to him!" Marta said, her impish face glowing like a Klieg light. "*¡Puta madre!* You spoke to your man! What did he say? Did you touch him? Did he touch you? Do you know what hotel room he's in?"

I still had not regained the ability of speech and could only turn to Marta with a triumphant grin. "I can die happy now."

"And the night is still young," Marta sighed. "I wonder where Dave is." I imagined the unshaven frontman still in his dressing room, staring into a mirror and congratulating himself on another triumphant performance.

"We need one more!" a voice boomed throughout the room. "One more. C'mon, mates, who knows how to play footie?" A tall, wild-eyed bloke with a crop of bushy hair stood in front of the foosball table, two mates on the other side waiting for him to score a partner.

I glanced around the room, but none of the other fans seemed to understand what the Irishman was blustering about.

I raised a timid hand. "You know footie?" the bloke asked, the amusement resounding in his voice.

"Just a little," I confessed.

"Whattaya know? The ginger Yank claims to know footie." His mates around the table swigged their beer in hearty gulps and laughed at my expense. "Well, what yer waiting for? We need a fourth."

"You know who they are?" Marta whispered as I began to walk over.

"Roadies?"

"No, that's the *opening band.*" She looked frightened, as if my next moves would decide our fate for the rest of the tour. "I hope you learned something at that college in Michigan." I shrugged her hand off my shoulder, an attempt to boost my confidence as all the eyes in the room watched the ginger American prat take her place at the foosball table with the members of Marxman.

"I'm Hollis," my partner said. "This here's Jimmy and Tommy." Up close, I now recognized them as the lead singer, whistle player, and bassist, respectively. Marta brought me another beer, "for luck," and I took a violent swig.

"Let's just make sure we play by the same rules on this side of the Pond," Hollis said. "Actually, there's only one rule: no spinning."

That much I knew. "Of course." I raised a beer to toast our good luck. "Let's cream 'em."

By now the majority of the backstage occupants had gathered around the table to watch, mainly because they'd all hoped to get a good laugh at the female—American, at that—who thought she knew something about footie. That much I discerned from the snatches of Spanish I overheard, and more than once I saw Marta shoot an icy stare at a chipper making derogatory comments. It was like having my own security guard, or at least my own pitbull-cum-PR rep.

The first game, I did a remarkable job on offense, slamming home three goals against Jimmy's blank-eyed stare. "You see that!" a wild-eyed Tommy roared, slapping his partner on the shoulder. "The bird just schooled you."

Dark-haired, green-eyed Jimmy gave me a mock evil eye. "You, girlie, are getting yours." Our opponents scored two more before Hollis, from the other end of the table, knocked in two. A moment later and it was over, Hollis and I having just edged out our challengers.

"We won?" I said, incredulously.

"Not yet," Tommy said, forcing another beer into my hand. "Best outta three."

For the next two games, I did my best not to spin, no matter how frustrated I became, and tried to ignore the small crowd that had gathered about the table. I didn't even look up when Marta whispered that Fletch and Martin had joined the throng.

Despite our best efforts, Hollis and I fared worse in the next two games, losing by only a point or two, but losing nonetheless. I gave Hollis a sheepish "Sorry."

"No worries," he said. "When you walked over, I expected a downright slaughter. At least I got one in on 'em. You can be my footie mate anytime." He raised his beer bottle, gave me a quick "cheers," then went and joined his bandmates.

I ran my hand over the side of the foosball table. If only I'd known how handy such a skill could be, I would have spent twice as much time at Tau Gamma Nu, where a free table awaited at any given hour, rather than wasting time reading Abelard woo Heloise. I silently thanked the skewered plastic men on the table and would have shook each of their hands, had they not been molded to the sides of their bodies.

I sensed Marta standing next to me, waiting to break my reverie. "You didn't ask him for tickets," she said with an uncharacteristic tone of caution. "It was the perfect opportunity."

I shook my head and noticed that the room, although not my vision, had cleared. I usually paced my drinking, but I'd been too intent on my game to turn down any bottle passed into my hand. "I thought we had tickets for Madrid and Barcelona. Why would I ask for others?" It hadn't even occurred to me to hit up anyone in Marxman, and I had to admit it wouldn't have been overly awkward, had I considered it.

"Yes, but... it would have been brilliant to have our names on the guest list, no?" She cocked her head, a tad chagrined yet appreciative of the latent talents she'd just witnessed.

I conceded as much, but shrugged. "It was a brilliant evening all around."

"Positively brilliant."

"*¡La puta madre!*"

Smiling at my use of her favorite phrase, Marta grabbed my hand as security ushered us out. I wasn't comfortable with such a public display of affection—from a male, let alone a female—but I passed it off as a European trait when I recalled how Marion would often weave my arm through hers, even while strolling the streets of Manhattan.

We walked into the warm night air, cool by the standards of the stifling backstage room, and Marta took a deep breath. "Can you believe the night?" She spun around like a schoolgirl, letting go of my hand only to pirouette, then grip it close again. We strolled along a service drive at the back of the arena, deserted except for two inebriated groupies high on the experiences of the past few hours. "It was a perfect night, yes. Perfect. As you said, *la puta madre.*"

The uneven pavement joined forces with my innate lack of grace and drunken state to cause me to stumble, but Marta caught me. "Did you drink too much, Zhane?"

I laughed, remembering the time I'd drank half a fraternity under a table and still managed to clean up in pool. "Too much? No. Just enough, I would think. I'm just a natural klutz."

Marta held me a little closer, as if she didn't quite buy my alibi. "Shh." She stopped in her tracks and motioned in front of her. A few yards ahead, silhouetted in the streetlights that lay just beyond the arena gates, a bear of a man staggered, pausing to swig from a bottle every few steps. "Let's wait until he leaves the gate. Then we'll go." We watched as he made it to the fence surrounding the arena, took a final gulp, then tossed the bottle behind him without looking. It crashed at our feet, sending splatter and shards flying in the halogen light.

I must have caught my breath—Marta would later claim I belched—because the figure turned around and came rushing towards us, his head lowered like a charging bull. "You!" he grunted, his wild hair diffusing the light behind him. "You!" Marta and I stayed our ground as he neared. A moment later his face was illuminated and I recognized the wild Irish eyes. "You play a pretty mean game of footie… for a bird." It was Tommy, half of the team that had delivered me a can of whoop-ass thirty minutes earlier. He was considerably drunker than last we'd seen him.

"Thanks. I think."

"Right, thanks. Of course." He seemed to take in the sight of two lone "birds" in an alley, but I was hardly worried. We were only a hundred yards from the backstage door and, with Tommy in such a state, it wouldn't have taken an Olympian to outrun his 250-pound frame. "You two want to…" He swayed and steadied himself. Of all the times I'd imagined being propositioned by a musician—semi-famous or otherwise—none of them had been remotely like this. "You want to go on a pub crawl?"

That wasn't quite what I'd expected to come out of the Irish bear's mouth, but it was much more pleasant than the alternatives. "Pub crawl?" Just the sound of those words spoken with an Irish accent were so much more exotically seductive than the nasally "bar hop" I was accustomed to hearing back home. I turned to Marta. "What time is our train tomorrow?"

"Late, very late." She dismissed my worries by turning to Tommy. "We'd love to. This is my hometown. I know a wonderful place."

Tommy's eyes shone like beacons. "Brilliant! But it would be great if it could be nearby." When he mentioned that he hoped to crawl home to his hotel, my heart flipped at the name.

Any qualms I'd had about shucking out 5,000 pesetas for our accommodations flew out the window. Our temporary digs had us staying amongst peers, friends. Nay, footie mates.

"There's a place just a few blocks from there," Marta said, glad to once again take charge. "Come, I'll show you."

Tommy hooked his arms through both of ours so that Marta and I bookended him, a ragtag group off to stagger down our own Yellow Brick Road. "You gals shouldn't be wandering the streets alone. Lots of nutters out there."

We holed up in a small pub, Tommy ordering the first round. "You up for a rematch?" He hooked a wild eye over at the foosball table in the corner.

I raised my beer bottle in the now obligatory salute. "You're on."

Marta approached, her autographed ticket extended in her hand. "Here, I don't have pockets. Will you hold this for me? It's signed by all of them… except Dave."

I held up my hands, not wanting to be put in charge of such an important strip of paper. "No way. I'm not just a klutz, I lose things, too."

"You have pockets. That gives you a better chance than me, even if you are a loser." I didn't think Marta quite grasped the true meaning of that word, but I let it slide. "Tuck it into that pouch you have." She reached under my shirt, where I'd thought I'd securely hidden my little black travel satchel, and shoved it in there. "Now, let's kick some Irish ass."

With only three players, Marta—who I put on the offense, as I could score just as well on defense while still manning the goal—and I played against Tommy who, although drunker than a sailor on leave, still managed some frighteningly accurate shots with his goalie. Each time the ball thwacked home, he'd give a hearty roar, rousing his already wild hair. But Marta and I, our wits still half-conscious, held our own and declared victory.

"A fine game," Tommy declared. "Fine playing. Another round!" He hoisted his empty bottle in the air as a signal for the barkeep.

By the third game, I was swaying and barely able to keep the ball in focus. Luckily for me and Marta, Tommy was having as much trouble just gripping the handles and only caught Marta spinning every fifth time. "Spinning!" he'd yell and point an accusatory finger. "Redo! Spinning!"

He chatted us up, and Marta did her best to decipher his slurred Irish brogue as he related tales on the road and the merits of musicianship. Between goals—we hardly kept score anymore, mainly because our capacity to count had been diluted by cervezas—we swapped stories of drunken misadventures, Tommy's always trumping our plebian tales. He bellowed with amusement as I told him of my March mishap at a certain fraternity where I got caught in a hot tub by my date's girlfriend and had my hair freeze and then break when my sister wanted to test its frozen elasticity.

"You can't trust blokes," Tommy lectured, wagging a hairy finger. "Not even me. Remember that."

"You seem alright," I insisted, trying to keep the conversation from going downhill. Drunken camaraderie with males was my forte. I enjoyed being one of the guys and aimed to keep it that way with this one.

"Can't trust 'em." He finished another beer. I imagined he was largely responsible for keeping the Guinness brewery open. "But you birds are alright, even for Yanks."

"I'm not a Yank." Marta seemed positively livid that Tommy had not noticed her lack of forehead signage. "I'm from here, Pontevedra. This is my hometown."

Our Irish comrade brushed off her contempt with a wave of his paw. It amazed me that hands his size could so deftly manage a bass guitar. "Ain't nothing wrong with Yanks, mind you. Just saying that my 'speriences with 'em haven't been so pleasant up till now. You Yanks locked?"

I gathered by the context that he was asking how drunk we were. "Quite locked."

"Eh, yeah." He drew a hand down his face, as if to purge the drink within him. "We leave for Madrid early tomorrow. Best be getting back to the hotel." He clapped a hand on my back. "You're alright for a Yank."

He wove his way to the door and held it open for us. "M'ladies." Marta and I locked arms for balance and tumbled out of the tavern. Tommy followed close enough behind that I could feel his breath bluster between us with each step he took. Within a block, he'd taken to singing Irish ballads at the top of his mighty lungs, his voice reverberating through the empty streets.

We tottered across a pedestrian bridge, in the middle of which Tommy stopped to sing a rousing chorus of friendship and drink. His full-bellied chortle filled the air, threatening to wake up the town, if not level entire city blocks. My ninth-grade Spanish teacher had instilled in me romantic visions of Spanish serenades, but I bet she'd never imagined my first would be from a drunken Irishman.

The last few beers were having an effect on me and I was having a difficult time keeping my eyes from crossing. Out-drinking frat boys was one thing, and I'd always credited that talent to my heritage—Irish, Russian, and German, cultures so intent with perfecting intoxication that they'd squeezed alcohol from all manner of foodstuffs, including the humble potato. Pub-crawling with a genuine 18-stone Irishman was quite another league altogether.

So it was no surprise that not a single one of us heard the stranger on the bridge approach, nor that none of us quite remembered what happened the next day. What Marta and I did recall from our collective memories was that the interloper, a Spaniard equally as smashed as any of us, wanted me to go with him to a bar. I had no such intentions—my only thoughts were of my soft, 5,000-peseta bed just across the street. But the Spaniard was insistent, and no argument from Marta was going to dissuade him. Even my now-rote "*No hablo español*" didn't keep him from blathering away in ninety-mile-per-hour Gallego.

Tommy's argument, however, would be another matter, and when I saw his eyes blaze fire, his hair seemingly take on a life of its own as he got a bead on the scrawny Spaniard who barely came up to my shoulder, I knew, even with my eyeballs floating in brew, that this could not possibly end well. As I tried to tell the Spaniard in the most horrible Spanish ever spoken that I was so very, very uninterested in going anywhere at that moment—"*No puedo hacer nada, excepto dormir. Sí, dormir. Quiero dormir ahora, ahora exactamente*"—I spied Tommy charging towards us. An image of the lumbering Irishman lifting the stranger like an old tire and flinging him over the side of the bridge flashed through my mind. I still had two concerts to go to. There was no way I was going to miss them for jail time or a prolonged discussion with Interpol.

I put myself between Tommy and the Spaniard. "*Espera.* Marta, tell him to wait."

"You just did."

"Exactly." I spun around to Tommy and, certain the diminutive stranger couldn't understand English, much less our slurred dialect, I told the Behemoth of an Irishman my plan. "Look, there's a bar just across the street. I'll go there with him, order a drink, then say I have to go to the bathroom—which really isn't a lie." I listed to one side and one of Tommy's great hands righted me. "Then, when he thinks I'm going to the bathroom, I'll sneak out." I pantomimed sneaking, not worrying if Spaniards would understand charades or Hanna-Barbera impersonations. "I'll leave him there, like that!" I attempted a snap and impressed myself when I heard the sound.

Tommy put two meaty hands on my shoulders. "You sure about this? I can just toss him—"

"No, no tossing." I shook my head emphatically and immediately regretted doing so. "I can do this." I flung my shoulders back and stood as tall as I could manage. "I'm a New Yorker. I can handle myself."

Marta pulled me aside, out of earshot of both men. "I do not think this is a good idea, Jenn."

I hiccupped. "You said my name. You should drink more often."

"This is not safe." She held both my hands and looked at me imploringly. Inebriation had softened her face so that she looked as cuddly as a green-eyed kitten. "I do not want to leave you. That's it. I will not leave you."

I stroked the side of her soft kitty face. "I'll be okay. I have a confession to make. I'm in a sorority. You know what that means?"

"You sleep with many men?"

"Not that good a sorority. No, it means I know how to fend off drunks. Look, if I'm not back in fifteen minutes, you can call the sheriff."

There is nothing so convincing as drunken appeals. Within moments I was sauntering into the bar across the street, Marta holding Tommy back lest he should decide to make the Spaniard into a tortilla.

My stalker and I hadn't been sitting long before I attempted my escape. I held up a finger to halt his next attempt at English. "*El baño. Necesito el baño.*"

I rose and got my bearings. I was rather certain the bathrooms were behind me, but freedom lay in the opposite direction. I took a chance that *el stalkero* was too drunk to realize any differently. In the darkness of the bar, and in my current level of intoxication, I relied mainly on touch to get me around the corner and over to the front door of the bar, which if memory serves correctly, would have been a wonderfully romantic place to visit with someone who wasn't a sexual predator. Dark wood, dim lighting, and wall sconces provided the medieval setting from which I now attempted to free myself, but I was so sated with mead that I couldn't figure out how to work the door to the dungeon. I peeked around the corner to see if my would-be molester was watching, but he merely sipped his beer, his back still to me. I jiggled the knob a few more times but still could not manage to get out.

Alcohol has a way of warping all sense of time, so I could very well have been struggling to leave the bar for five minutes or five hours, I had no clue. But after a while, *el stalkero* came hunting and found me about to rip the door off its hinges. Just as he tried to slip an arm around my waist, the door flung open and I took off as fast as my gelatinous legs would carry me. My diminutive suitor followed, imploring me with slurred speech and pawing gestures to return with him—either to the bar or his home, I wasn't sure. I'd shrug off his hand, only to find it suddenly glued to my waist. When I'd reached the door to the hotel lobby I turned to face him and, in the best Spanish I could muster, informed him that I was leaving, and that if he even thought about stepping foot inside, I would not hesitate to take drastic measures. The word *policía* made several appearances in my speech, but I refrained from mentioning abuse to his *cojones,* figuring that threats would only incite anger.

Before walking through the doorway, I pointed at the spot where the stalker stood and, as if he were a hound, told him to stay. He gazed up at me with soft brown eyes, and for a moment I thought he might begin blubbering right there. I entered the hotel, casting a reproachful glance over my shoulder.

Despite my warnings, the little bastard followed me in, but before I could make good on my words, Marta had wedged herself between us and unleashed a verbal lashing that made me cringe, even though

I only understood a smattering. Any time the stalker even so much as opened his mouth, Marta lit into him, standing on her tiptoes as the barrage of words poured forth. She shoved his chest a few times, a brazen move that even I hadn't dared, and forced him backwards to the door, which she held open for him.

"*¡Vaya!*" she commanded, shoving him into the street as the concierge looked on with a look of startled disbelief.

"*¡Sin dios!*" I called after him, even braver now that I had backup.

As soon as the stalker was out of sight, Marta took my hand in both of hers, nearly crushing it. "Jenn, I am so glad you're okay. I was just coming to get you." She sounded more like a concerned parent than my peer and partner-in-crime.

"I'm fine, just had some technical difficulties." Perhaps Marta had feared that she'd be implicated in anything that might have happened to me. I couldn't have imagined her showing such concern a few hours earlier.

"Come." She led me to the elevator. "Tommy is worried. We must tell him you're okay. He asked that you come see him so that he could see with his own eyes."

I slumped against the elevator wall, no longer able to contain my exhaustion. "I have to get to bed, Marta. Help me swim there."

"I promised him," she said. "Here is the floor." She took my hands and led me from the elevator and down the hall, my feet dragging on the carpet and my head flopping from one shoulder to the other. Once outside Tommy's room, she propped me against the wall before knocking. A voice beckoned us inside.

I held fast to the doorjamb as I stuck my head inside the veritable hotel room of a rock star. Tommy lay prone on the bed, still in his clothes. Next to him sat Paul the drummer, watching some horrid late-night program on Spanish public access. "You must be Tommy's drinking buddies. He told me all about you. Was worried, he was." He elbowed Tommy gently in the gut. "Hey, bloke. Your birds are back."

Tommy flinched and managed to open his eyes into narrow slits. "Yer alright."

I nodded, and immediately regretted the unnecessary movement. "Fine."

"'Sgood." His head sunk back into the pillow and the snoring commenced.

"Yer the footie player, aincha?" Tommy's annoyingly sober mate asked. "You ain't bad. Not bad at all."

My grip on the doorjamb began to slip and Marta kept me from falling all the way over. "Thanks." I knew I'd be fine as long as I kept my sentences short and monosyllabic.

Marta took over conversational duties. "I think we should get some sleep. It was nice meeting you." She threw one of my arms over her shoulder and began to close the door.

"Join us for breakfast, won't you?" Paul called. "Eleven o'clock downstairs. Bus leaves just after that."

It was already nearly five in the morning. "We'll be there," Marta promised. "*Buenas noches.*"

I assume that Marta was the one who tucked me into bed that night. When I awoke the next morning, I was still clothed—same outfit I'd sweated in while waiting in line, cheered in at the concert, and partied in all night long. While Marta slept, I hopped into the shower and cleansed myself of some of the previous day's festivities. But when I dug into my backpack, I found that I'd forgotten to pack my toothbrush. I cursed myself for leaving behind such an important item—I never felt fully awake until I'd brushed my teeth—but was glad it was something that was cheap and easily replaced. The fuzz that had accumulated on my teeth would have to remain there until I'd once again visited the *farmacia*.

But when Marta finally roused, all such plans of toothbrush shopping were dashed. "It's 11:30!" she exclaimed. "Why didn't you wake me?"

I tried sucking the schmutz off my teeth. "This is the first good sleep we've gotten in days. A full five hours—in beds, no less. I wasn't going to bother you."

"Bother me?" Marta had hopped out of bed. "Zhane, the band is waiting downstairs for us. They leave soon." I noted how Marta's pronunciation of my name had reverted and wondered if her fluency had dried up with the alcohol. After a few moments of bustling around throwing on clothes, she put her hands to her temples. "How is it you look so rested?" Her bloodshot eyes met mine and I realized my Spanish amiga had a bit of a hangover.

"Slept. Took a shower. All good." I touched up my lipgloss in the bathroom mirror. "You want to shower before we go downstairs?"

Marta had ducked under the bed in search of an errant shoe. "No time. They may already have left." She ran a brush through her hair, rubbed her fingers across her teeth, and declared herself ready.

When we reached the lobby restaurant, all of Marxman were already eating, but not a single Depeche member was in sight. Marta tried not to appear crestfallen as we nonchalantly took seats at the counter. I'd just ordered a tall orange juice and toast when Tommy clapped a hand on my shoulder, a beer in his other hand. His eyes, while still wide and wild, were slightly less bloodshot than Marta's.

"Hair o' the dog," he greeted us, raising his pint and settling into the stool next to me, his large frame teetering on the tiny seat. "How you two feeling today?"

I shrugged. "Not so bad. A little tired, but it could be worse."

"No hangover?" Tommy seemed skeptical that an American bird could have survived the previous night's drinking without so much as a whimper.

I jabbed a thumb over my shoulder at my traveling companion, who had propped up her head with one hand and did her best not to nod off into her eggs. "I'm fine. Marta, however, could probably use a few more hours' sleep."

"I'll survive." She gave me a playful tap. "I don't know how this one is standing."

"It's the Irish in her," Tommy declared, squeezing my shoulder with his great mitts. "Sure ye don't want a pint?"

We gabbed for a few minutes, during which I filled Tommy in on my escape from the Spaniard. "I knew I should have tossed him off the bridge!" he roared when I mentioned how the stalker had gotten handsy. The three of us had a good laugh over our shenanigans, and Tommy invited us to do it again in Madrid. "I'll make sure you've got passes and tickets in Madrid, right?"

I could feel Marta's excitement even with my back to her. Once again, the rock gods had delivered without even being asked. While Tommy gave Keith, the tour director, our information so that the tickets would be waiting at will-call, Marta and I swapped wide-ass grins. We already had tickets to the shows, but now we had secured the ever-important backstage passes.

Tommy mentioned some last-minute tasks he had to take care of and began to excuse himself. As his six-foot bulk rose above us, he put a hand on each of our shoulders and nodded approvingly. "You two are alright. When you're done here in Spain, you should come to London and see us play there. You can stay in my flat."

I did my best not to appear overly excited as I thanked him and said goodbye. As soon as he had left the restaurant, Marta and I turned to conspire but were interrupted by Paul, who assumed Tommy's empty stool.

"Heard you had a right good pub crawl last night," he said. He was several inches shorter than Tommy, so I didn't have to crane my neck upwards to look him in the eye. "Wish I could join you on your next one."

"Join us in Madrid tomorrow night," I offered. I could only imagine what our drink-a-thon would be like once we got to the capital. "Not a bad life you've got—playing music, seeing new cities, partying every night."

Paul shrugged, his dark eyes a little somber. "Eh, it's not really for me."

"You serious?" I asked. Marta, having learned that Depeche Mode would not be joining us for our morning meal, had dropped out of the conversation, her head on the counter and nose inches away from some unidentifiable breakfast meat.

"Yeah, I'm not going to tour much more. I want to leave in a few days, maybe after Madrid." I couldn't imagine walking away from the life of a rock star, let alone a rock star who'd had the great fortune of landing an opening gig for the Greatest Band That Ever Was. If I'd had any sense of musical ability, I would have tried that route myself. But I played no instruments, and although I could carry a tune, the only thing my voice inspired was earplugs. When driving around in my Firebird, even I turned up the radio so that I couldn't hear myself sing. Had I been blessed with golden pipes, there was nothing that could have stopped me from pursuing rock idoldom.

Paul told me how he missed home, his family, and his neighborhood pub where they poured the best pints of Guinness outside of the Dublin brewery. He wove such a magical picture of his town that I made a mental note to visit one day, invitation or not.

"You miss your family?" Paul asked.

100

I shrugged. "Not really. I've only been gone a few days. Plus I don't see my family most of the year anyway since I'm away at school."

Paul looked at me with a knowing gaze. "You're one of those."

"One of what? A student?"

He shook his head at my foolishness. "Some people can leave home, no strings attached. It's that wanderlust, it gets 'em. Others can't stray more than a few blocks. I'll probably never move further than the next town over, and I'd be reluctant to do even that." He sighed as if having made his decision had eased him of a great burden. "I love my family. Being away from them gets me right here." He beat his breastbone with his fist. "I never really appreciated my family when I was home. Don't get me wrong, they know I love them. But being away from them has shown me what's really important. You can fuck all this rock-star shite. Just give me my family, a pint, and football, and I'm a happy man." He polished off the rest of his juice and stood up. "Nice chatting with you."

Paul moseyed off—if Irishmen could indeed mosey—leaving me with thoughts of home, a plate full of cold, flaccid eggs, and Marta dozing at my side. I nibbled a slice of toast, normally my favorite part of breakfast, and found it had lost its appeal. My stomach growled, demanding to be compensated for having endured the events of the previous night. The morning after a binge, I always rewarded myself with a hearty meal to calm the roiling liquids in the pit of my stomach. But the meal before me no longer seemed appetizing, so I concentrated on my orange juice, which had just a wee bit too much pulp for my liking.

"You two have become quite the center of conversation," said tour director Keith. I hadn't realized there'd been a queue to converse with us. The stool next to me was a rotating cast of characters, and my head was still so fuzzy—almost as fuzzy as my teeth—that I had trouble keeping track of everyone, let alone keeping up with conversation. "Now, Tommy tells me you're to be put on the list for the Madrid show, that right?"

"And Barcelona," I added.

"Right. Got it. Now, this how you spell your name?" I glanced at his notepad.

"Yeah, that's it. And her name is spelled—"

"I'll just put you down for a plus one, how's that?" He ticked off a number next to my name in a perfunctory fashion. From his too-peppy smile, I couldn't tell if he hated his job and was just being glib, or if he actually enjoyed the mundane minutiae, especially when it came to satisfying the demands of groupies of opening bands.

"It's too bad about Paul," I said, trying to make small talk. I gnawed the side of my toast, too hungry to deny my stomach the sustenance it so deserved.

"What's wrong with the bloke?" Keith asked. "He seemed all right when I spoke to him."

"Oh, he's fine. I just meant about him leaving the band and all." As I watched Keith's face morph from scout-leader chipper to all-out shock, I realized I'd just spilled the Heinz baked beans.

"Leaving the band? He ain't leaving the band!" Keith slapped his notepad against the counter. "Who says he's leaving the band? He ain't said nothing to me about it."

I wasn't sure exactly how colossal the secret I'd accidentally let loose was, but I was pretty certain it wasn't going to turn out favorably for me if I stuck around. I knew from past experience that the sooner I could remove myself from an unfavorable situation, the less likely anyone would be to connect me to the crime. "You know, I think I see him in the lobby. Perhaps you should talk to him yourself, talk him into staying." I nudged Marta, trying to jolt her awake so that we could make a break the first chance we got.

"Darn right I will. We've got a show tomorrow night." And Keith stormed off in search of his drummer.

"Marta, wake up." Her eyelids flickered. "We've gotta get out of here."

"Our train doesn't leave for another few hours." She pushed away the plate of untouched breakfast just as the waitress came over with our check and rattled off something in Spanish, which I assumed was her asking whether we were with the band. Marta and I exchanged quick glances, then in unison replied, "*Sí.*" The waitress apologized and took back the check. As we sneaked through the lobby, we could hear bellowing Irish voices echo down the halls, and I felt a twinge of guilt at whatever Paul was now facing.

"You think he's mad now," I whispered to Marta. "Just wait until he sees the check. It'll take him an hour to figure out who the hell ordered orange juice, of all things."

Back on the streets of Pontevedra, Marta and I recapped the previous night, filling each other in on events the other had missed. I told her about not being able to open a simple doorknob, while she relayed Tommy's fit in the hotel lobby and how the concierge had almost called the police.

"He reminds me of Slash," Marta told me, comparing Tommy to a member of Guns N' Roses. "The wild hair, the guitar. Except, of course, without the 'Made in America' sign on his forehead. And that ridiculous top hat. And the fact I like Tommy's music."

We strolled up and down hills, Marta pointing out the various sites. I didn't think it possible, but the sun seemed stronger than it had the previous day. Marta poked my skin to test how my tan was coming along. "Still white. We'll change that."

I began to recognize landmarks as we headed back to the train station. I'd seen so little of Pontevedra, the town Marta called home, but I was leaving with fond memories. Marta told me about the connection between Galicia and Ireland, how the "black Irish" were reputed to be descendants of shipwrecked Spanish sailors on the Emerald Isle's west coast. Because of this mixing, Marta claimed, there were great Celtic influences still evident in Galician life, and she herself felt a great affinity with the Irish. "One day," she said, "I will live in Ireland."

Silence followed our uphill trudging, and light-hearted banter took us back down. Something had changed between Marta and me. No longer was I the helpless foreigner who needed my Spanish guide for tasks as simple as ordering a meat-free meal. It was my talents, questionable as they were, that had gotten us backstage, my native English skills and foosball acumen that had made us the standouts of the backstage party.

As for Marta, her boldness in chasing off el stalkero had shown me a side of her I hadn't expected. I'd wrongly, and unjustly, assumed that her forthright behavior and desire to lead had precluded her of any emotions that would allow the building of an equitable friendship. But I could clearly recall the expression on her face, both during and after she'd chased away el stalkero, and the emotions I'd seen there were clearly benevolent, not simply those of someone hoping to reap the benefits of my Bong card and footie skills.

We reached the deserted train station and parked ourselves under the awning out of the sunlight. The train wouldn't come for several hours, but Marta had wanted to leave town lest a family member see her and report back to her parents. She soon excused herself and went inside to call Julio.

When she returned, she looked flustered. "We cannot go home." She said this more plainly than if she'd found the Coke machine to be out of order. Our plan had been to return to León, introduce me to the parental units—who believed I was arriving that day—then grab Marta's younger brother, Estevo, and return to Madrid for the concert. However, recent events in the Paredes household had changed our itinerary. "We're going straight to Madrid. How do you say it? The cat is out of the sack."

She proceeded to tell me how Julio had relayed the information that her parents knew that I was already in Spain, that Sabina had called and accidentally let loose that pertinent piece of information that we both were in Pontevedra when Marta was supposed to be at a friend's in Madrid awaiting my arrival. *Los padres* Paredes were so furious at having been lied to that they had decided that when Marta came home, they would not allow her—and, therefore, me—to attend the Madrid concert. Since this was inconceivable to Marta, especially since we'd already secured backstage passes, we would go directly to the capital. "Either way," Marta rationalized, "Estevo would not see the concert. At least this way we still can."

I hadn't met Estevo and, although I was certain he was a swell hombre, I didn't give a rat's ass that he wouldn't be seeing the Madrid show. As long as I was there, backstage pass affixed proudly to my chest, I'd be the happiest girl in all *España*.

Although Marta didn't ask for my consent for these plans, I wouldn't have argued. I couldn't imagine missing out on the Madrid show, which was to be held in a bullring, the aptly named Plaza de Toros. I'd already experienced such anguish on two previous occasions:

the aforementioned *101* premiere in Manhattan, and a few years prior to that when the band had held auditions for the film.

I told Marta of the first incident, how tryouts had been held at the Malibu nightclub in Lido Beach, less than twenty miles from my Long Island home. I'd just seen Depeche at the Jones Beach amphitheater and was wearing the concert t-shirt when I heard the news announced on WDRE, a local radio station often credited with breaking many of the bands that have since become synonymous with the 1980s and alternative music. I had planned on skipping school, catching a bus down to Lido, and proving to the casting director that, although I'd seen Depeche Mode live only once (and that only a few days prior), I was indeed their biggest fan and therefore could not be denied access on the bus that would follow the band around the country.

"That was the Music for the Masses tour, 1988," Marta said with a quizzical gaze. "You were maybe 14 years old? I remember looking into airfares until I found out the minimum age was 18."

"But I had my sister's driver's license." I raised an impish brow. "As far as the casting director would have been concerned, I was 25."

Marta laughed so hard she nearly fell off the bench. "I thought *I* was bad," she said.

"Yeah, well, I didn't make it to the auditions. My mom found out my plans and kept me home until it was too late for me to even try. Then she dropped me off at school just in time for my least favorite class, earth science. I remember 'mourning' and wearing all black for weeks afterward. Actually, I think that's when my all-black, all-the-time phase began."

"That makes it two times then."

"What do you mean?"

"Two times your mom prevented you from meeting Depeche Mode. That was the first, the second was the premiere."

I hadn't actually thought of it that way, that it had been my mother who'd kept me from meeting them. And she'd tried to prevent this occurrence, too, but the third time had proven a charm. I even had proof tucked away in the travel pouch around my neck. I reached in for my and Marta's tickets, but could only find one. Try as I might, I couldn't keep my rummaging a secret from Marta and soon she was asking what I was searching for.

After a few moments, I gave a resigned sigh and confessed: I had only one of our autographed tickets. I refrained from saying I'd warned her that I lose things, but Marta came up with a creative solution, one that I reluctantly agreed to. "When we are backstage tomorrow night, you can get your autographs again. But this ticket"—she held up the lone survivor of our drunken evening—"is from the concert in my hometown. I must keep this one." She tucked it away in her bra, her favorite repository of treasured items large and small.

I took the time to sort through the rest of my travel pouch and made another depressing discovery. "Uh, I didn't happen to lend you 10,000 pesetas last night, did I?"

Marta furrowed a brow. "I do not think we drank *that* much, no."

"Crap. Then some lucky duck is probably buying his friends rounds in celebration of finding your ticket." Hoping I'd stored it separately from my at-hand stash, I felt in my super-secret location for the rest of the wad my father had given me, and began counting it out. I hadn't considered the effect it would have on Marta.

"Is that… is that your spending money?" Marta's eyes were wider than when she'd thought Martin was singing in our hallway.

"Uh, yeah."

She paused before asking the next question. "All of it?"

I didn't know whether or not I should answer that question honestly, but decided it didn't really matter either way. "No, I left some in the Suitcase From Hell, just in case."

Marta looked away while I counted the bank. "I don't want to be nosy, but it looks like you have about 300,000 pesetas there. It's not safe to travel with that kind of money. Not like that. What if someone stole it all?"

"Then I have this." I whipped out my father's American Express card. "He called ahead to the company to give me permission. But I'm only supposed to use it for emergencies."

As soon as the words had left my mouth, I wondered what Marta would constitute an emergency: Drinks for the band? Doubles of every concert tee? A five-star hotel in Madrid and Barcelona, separate rooms for each of us?

Back home, my friends knew how I felt about money. All through high school and now into college, I'd kept a part-time job, despite my father's urgings to quit. For the basic necessities, I'd gone to him— food, clothing, school, summer educational programs. But for all my entertainment—movies, concerts, posters, and, of course, music—I'd used my own money, earned at various restaurants between Long Island and Michigan. By the time I'd gone to Spain, I estimated that I'd spent roughly $4,000 of my own money on Depeche Mode memorabilia—no small feat considering my take-home wage averaged five dollars an hour working at a takeout Chinese restaurant in high school.

Having my own income—and doing with it what I pleased— provided me with a sense of independence. If I wanted an album, I didn't have to explain to my mom or dad why I was asking for money, I'd just dip into my own funds. I'd even saved up for this trip, though the pittance in my piggy bank was nothing compared to what my father had bankrolled.

The night before I left for Europe, the Twelve Apostles came over my house for a send-off. By the time my father returned home well after midnight, only my friend John remained. As my father sat me down at the dinette table, the location of many a midnight lecture on my future, he explained to me why this trip was so important. "Experiencing other cultures will broaden your mind!" he declared. "Right now, you brain is like a sponge. You have to soak up as much knowledge as you can!" That, he clarified, was the reason he was forking out such a wad.

On occasion—a school ski trip to Quebec, summer programs at the local college—my father had entrusted me with large sums of cash, an extra reward for my high grades and dedication to continual learning. But never before had there been a witness to such extravagances. I asked my father if he'd rather wait until we were alone, but he seemed to enjoy John's presence, reveling in his paternal ability to provide for his daughter.

As my father slowly counted out the hundreds, I noted John's reaction out of the corner of my eye. He remained silent through the whole transaction. My father wasn't giving me an open account that the teens of the illustrious North Shore of Long Island were allotted on a regular basis, but the amount he'd given me was sizable in terms of petty cash for those of my peer group. When my father retired for the night, John, my trustworthy friend through all my years of high school, had trouble looking me in the eye.

"Is that really your spending money?" His tone was foreign to me.

"No, it's for other things, too," I lied. "I'm sure he'll ask for the remainder when I return, or tell me next semester that part of this was intended for tuition."

Money had always made me insecure. Our family's financial standing fluctuated often due to my father's precarious career choice. At an early age I'd learned the value of a dollar, suckering my older siblings into paying several dollars to Café Jenn for homemade PB&J when they were under the influence, a physical condition I'd learned to recognize since the time I was in grade school. My mother was forever trying to make ends meet, even when my father was bringing home presents to me and my friends ("A dozen Swatches fell off the back of a truck!") on a nightly basis. It wasn't until junior high that I gleaned the truth of his income.

Because of recent events, I felt a kinship with Marta that I'd only previously experienced in what I referred to as "intensive living" situations—sleepaway camp, college orientation, etc.—and so shared some of my more intimate familial secrets, realizing that even if she leaked my stories, it would be only to those on another continent who would never know me. For the first time since I'd met her, Marta remained stoically silent, listening intently to my most personal family tales. She interrupted only in the very beginning, one of the few times she ever asked for a translation.

"What is a 'bookie'?"

I started from the beginning—the one I knew, at least.

When my father and mother married back in the early '70s, my father's side of the family owned a prominent Manhattan flower warehouse that had been in the family for decades. I had faint memories of running through fragrant, refrigerated rooms stocked with radiant blooms, an elevated train growling past just outside the main Brooklyn warehouse. By the time I was in kindergarten, my father, too proud to ask for any sort of financial compensation, had had a falling-out with his older brothers and walked away from the family business that my grandfather, who had died well before I was born, had founded. My uncles, of whom I had only the vaguest of memories, would go on to sell the business and properties to retire in affluent Florida beach towns.

With his livelihood cut off, my father turned to real estate to make ends meet. He had a modicum of success in this arena, but his desire to appease anyone and everyone proved both an asset and a deficit in a business that relied heavily on interpersonal relations. When the real estate market faltered, he looked to other avenues to supplement his income.

Although I was too young to pinpoint exactly when my father changed gears from legit career man to illicit entrepreneur, I later figured that it was some time when I was in kindergarten. That was around the time we went on a trip to Cape Cod with my cousins, and the parental units of the family, not trusting the others, employed me as the banker in their games of Monopoly.

As one of the greatest lovers of bacon in the Tri-State area, my father was perhaps the worst specimen of Jew to be found, but he loved poking fun at the heritage he revered, even going so far as to tell me, once I was in high school, that I couldn't be buried in the family plot because of my multiple piercings. I found it ironic that he would make such indictments while consuming a half-pound of pan-fried pork, which he washed down with a glass of milk. But pointing out such inconsistencies would only land me an extra half hour of Midnight Lectures, the designation I gave to his late-night pontifications on the importance of family, discipline, and, most importantly, education.

When I was in junior high, I kept my family relations to myself, save for a few close friends. My half-siblings, Janys and Ray, had attended the same high school a decade before, and their exploits were renowned; I was saved from association by the good fortune of different last names. Late in ninth grade, my blood ties were leaked, and several of my once-favorite teachers turned on me. Several other teachers gasped when they learned that their pet student—I'd never earned less than an A in any class—was related to their greatest nightmare, either Janys or Ray, depending on the instructor.

However, this aversion to my siblings was tempered by the fact that my halls of learning were less than 500 yards from my father's place of earning. Should my friends require a meal laden with MSG, I need only cross two streets to the premier Chinese restaurant on the Island and sign the back of a check to reap the benefits of my dad's acquaintances.

This was all well and good until I tried out for the softball team. Janys had often spun wild tales of her after-school activities with her favorite teachers, and Mr. Scarfone, a name that had cropped up often in her stories, was the head coach for varsity softball. After a few weeks on junior varsity, I attended a non-mandatory varsity session and was soon promoted to starting varsity pitcher. I thought nothing of it until Janys reminded me of Scarfone's connections to my father. "We used to get stoned under the bleachers," she told me. "Then we'd cross the street to Gum Ying and Scarfone would lay down a wad on the underdog." My father didn't have the heart to gouge the wallet of his stepdaughter's teacher, so Scarfone rarely walked away with empty pockets. However, when I learned of my coach's earlier transgressions, I couldn't help but think that my father's sway held some weight in the varsity lineup. By junior year, I'd used a car accident as an excuse to quit softball altogether.

My father's Jewish heritage—amongst other things—precluded him from being a heavyweight Mafia type. Although he may have had the most peripheral of dealings with true Mafioso, my father was only a bit-name player, forever hoping for a piece of the pie to which he could never lay claim. He was the most incongruent—and yet multicultural—of players: a Jew working for Italians out of a Chinese restaurant.

When Uncle Joe, as he was known among the Gum Ying clan, came, I often did my best to avoid him, knowing that the vodka martinis he'd imbibed would make him ripe for a Midnight Lecture. If he was feeling particularly anxious to proselytize for a few hours, my father would bust into the TV room and summon me to the dinette table. There, while Dad finished his bacon sandwich, he'd bluster until red in the face, extolling the virtues of higher education, and haranguing me as if I'd ever had the gall to bring home so much as a B on a pop quiz.

During one particular lecture, my father decided to take up the subject of my desire to be a writer. With bloodshot eyes and vapors of gin and tonic rolling off him like waves at high tide, he showered me with as much uninvited counsel as he did spittle, imploring me all the time to study, study, study. Then, prodding me on my sternum with his finger, he intoned, "Call. Me. Ishmael."

The look of confusion on my face, which he had probably hoped for, must have shown, because my father launched into a diatribe unlike any I'd heard before. Had I not known any better, I would have thought he'd rehearsed it. "*That*," he said waving his index finger heavenwards, "is the greatest opening line to any book ever. *That* is what you as a writer need aspire to. *That* is the caliber of writing I am expecting of you. Nothing less. I'm not keeping up this house just for show," he said, gesturing at the outdated wallpaper and yellow linoleum floor that would have embarrassed the Brady Bunch. "This is all for *you*. I work for *you*. And in return, I expect only the best. Do you understand?"

He then launched into his favorite joke parable, which I've since heard many times, only with a father-son cast: A daughter comes home from school and reluctantly hands her father a report card riddled with Cs. "Cs! I didn't raise my daughter to be a C student. What kind of student are you that you can only get Cs? And what kind of school are my taxes paying for that would allow you to get a C?" The daughter returns to school, vowing to work harder to please her father. The next quarter, she returns, a smug smile on her face as she hands over a report card full of Bs. "Bs!" shouts the father. "I didn't raise my daughter to be a B student. And what kind of school are my taxes paying for that you're so dumb you only get Bs?" The daughter once again trudges away, determined that this time she will not let her father down. When she returns with a report card full of straight As the next quarter, she's unprepared for his her father's response: "As! How awful is this school that even my daughter can get As?"

After such a talk, I'd often cry myself to sleep—not because of my dislike for being lectured, but because I was reminded that those rare moments were the only personal time my father and I ever spent together. Sure, we'd once visited the Coney Island Aquarium when I was in junior high (only because I called him on the Gum Ying pay phone crying that I never saw him), and from time to time I'd spy him in the stands at a volleyball or softball game, hooting and hollering like a walrus any time I so much as looked at the ball. But the truth of the matter was I didn't know my father. In fact, it wasn't until I was in junior high, around the time the Midnight Lectures began, that I even knew he'd graduated from Cornell.

I never gave much thought to the actual words of my father's blustering, and rarely did I think of what his daily dealings might entail. To my knowledge, I'd never met any of his non-real estate "co-workers" and, frankly, I didn't care to. I'd had enough run-ins with his "friends" that by the time I went to college my only wish was to get as far away as possible—if only to feel true independence by distancing myself from a community all too willing to go out of its way to cater to Uncle Joe and his clan. My dream had been to attend UCLA, but my father had put the kibosh on any inner-city schools—I'd be too distracted, he claimed—and I, in protest, refused to apply to his alma mater. But Michigan was far enough away, I figured, that the influence of Uncle Joe's friends wouldn't reach me.

After one particular incident, I'd even considered a college in Alaska, despite my aversion to the cold. John and I had driven in my beloved Firebird to a far-flung (by Long Island standards) town that none of us had ever visited, stopping at a local pizza joint to refuel. Our orders placed, we sat down to wait, but I was continually distracted by the guy behind the counter, who kept throwing an eyeball our way. Finally, he wagged a finger at me, saying, "I know you." I felt my stomach sink before his words even left his mouth. "You're Uncle Joe's daughter."

The pizza tosser proceeded to pull out a laminated newspaper clipping from beneath the counter and thrust it proudly towards me. "You pitched against Oceanside last week." I glanced at the plastic-coated newsprint and class photo my father had attached. I was wholly unsurprised when we were told the pizza was on the house. Being recognized by a total stranger was far more unnerving than having Melville spouted at me in the privacy of my own home.

Depending on my mood, I either indulged in or shunned the perks of my father's vocation. If I hadn't endured a Midnight Lecture in several months, I was more willing to treat a gaggle of friends to a small Polynesian feast, complete with flaming pu-pu platter. But if my father decided that a multi-night sermon was in order, I'd revolt and declare independence by dining at competing Chinese restaurants or filling up the Firebird at a gas station where the attendants didn't know my birthday.

One reason I never took the lectures to heart was because, deep down, I knew that my father was more bluster than brawn. He'd once had the brains to get a scholarship to Cornell, but he'd kept his intelligence masked for years beneath a gin-induced haze. I took umbrage at his bravado, my teenage self somehow sensing that his need to lecture came from his own beaten sense of self-worth. The respect he so craved from his bookie peers and clients could easily be forced from his daughter, the unwitting casualty of his floundering self-esteem.

Our relationship was never more precarious than when we visited Ann Arbor to decide if I should attend the University of Michigan. It was the first time we'd ever spent a night away from home, just the two of us, and my elation at visiting a Big Ten campus was tempered by my father's single-mindedness for academia, not to mention my mother's voice reminding me to keep an eye on his spending.

After surviving the flight, during which Uncle Joe refused to extinguish his cigarette despite the flight attendant's many requests, we drove into Ann Arbor, a liberal oasis in conservative "Militia-gan." At a stop sign, my father and I glanced about us, inhaling the spring air as if it were brimming with the knowledge and collegiate experience we both craved. Out my window, I spied two mop-haired frat boys playing frisbee on the roof of their house, a keg perched near the eaves. "Just as I'd pictured," my father's voice surprised me, echoing my thoughts.

But what sold my father on U of M was when he spied two Asian students, their arms overflowing with books, nattering in Italian. To him, the sight comprised everything university life should offer: studious mindsets coupled with the multiculturalism he embraced daily.

Despite my first impression of A-Squared's party atmosphere, I was still on the fence about attending, until the decision was made for me. My father, miffed and insulted that I hadn't been extended an invitation to the Honors College, marched up the steps of Angell Hall and demanded to know how his daughter could have been denied. When we left the office a half hour later, my fate had been sealed.

We celebrated my acceptance to the Honors College by dining in the darkly elegant Escoffier restaurant in The Bell Tower Hotel, where we were also staying. As my father ordered the most expensive steak on the menu, I tried not to think what my mother's reaction would be if she found the receipt. But that worry was soon dissipated when my father ordered a glass of wine for me, instructing the waiter not to "worry about details" (a phrase I thought he'd saved only for me) when I was asked to show ID. "You should learn to appreciate wine," he informed as he sipped his gin and tonic. "I want you to experience the finer things in life."

Thrilled with my newly acquired adult—and honors—status, I reveled in the moment, savoring our camaraderie as much as the elegant meal. The mushroom soup was beyond anything I'd ever tasted, and the aroma and texture remains imprinted in my memory to this day. My father and I chatted about the classes I would take, including Great Books, an honors-only class that had been the impetus for his trip to Angell Hall. We talked about possible majors and electives, study-abroad programs (he had high hopes for the Sorbonne), and extracurricular activities, including sororities. I hadn't expected my father to encourage me towards Greek life, until he told me how he felt that his college experience had been lacking due to not being in a fraternity. I was ambivalent, but my father saw compulsory sisterhood as a means to the finer things he'd wanted for me.

When he ordered his second gin and tonic, I reminded him of his promise to keep it to a two-drink maximum, and he assured me it would be his last. But after another half hour of feasting and conversing, his face already reddened and his eyes taking on a Midnight Lecture glow, he ordered another, and the discussion took a familiar precipitous turn. Over the soft tinkling of silverware on expensive china, my father's voice rumbled a bit too loud, like ominous thunder just over the hill. He warned me what would happen if I brought home a B, of how I must avoid party-seeking students who would distract me from my studies, of why a good, proper education was the most important asset I could bring with me into the real world four years hence. When I asked him to lower his voice because other patrons had turned to look, his face softened.

"I only want what's best for my little girl," he said, patting my hand in a highly uncharacteristic gesture of affection. "I only want the best. And I wanted to visit Ann Arbor to make sure you'd be safe here. I had to see for myself." His words chilled me, and I immediately began to wonder where he'd been all afternoon while I'd popped in and out of State Street with his American Express card. "I want you to know that you can always come to me. Always. And that you can *always* tell me the truth."

I was unused to wine, and the two glasses I'd downed had made me ripe for emotion. At these last words, my eyes stung and I heard my voice crack as I answered. "I will, Dad. I've never lied to you."

"I know you haven't." And, up to that point, I hadn't. His grip tightened on my hand and the dim lights of the chandelier reflected off his moistened eyes. "You're my little girl, and it's my job to watch after you. I know you get mad at me sometimes, but that's my job, to protect you and take care of you."

Swallowing had never been so difficult. I fought back the tears that threatened my mascara. "I'm not mad, it's just... it's just sometimes you go a little too far."

His grasp threatened to crush every single metacarpal even as the softness in his voice faded away. "I'm your father. There's no such thing as too far." With his free hand, he thrust a lecturing finger in my face. "Remember that. If I ever found out anyone hurt you, you know what I'd do?" His face contorted as he made a twisting motion with his hands. "I'd have 'em broken in half. Crushed. Then, poof!" He flitted his fingers like a magician dispersing smoke after vanishing a rabbit. "They'd never be seen again." He held my gaze, daring me to disbelieve his power. "Never."

He ordered another gin and tonic and continued to harangue me about my upcoming college years, which were looking bleaker by the moment. I had visions of Uncle Joe checking in with my professors, paying my roommates to act as moles, bugging the phone in my dorm room. He'd never gone to such lengths back home, but college was a "crucial time" for me, and I knew how much it meant to him that I not only succeed but rise above everyone around me. I declined my father's offer for a third glass of wine and pushed the half-eaten plate of food away. The elegance of the Escoffier seemed diminished, the chandeliers a little dimmer.

Perhaps due to the unusual environment—the posh ambiance, being alone with his youngest daughter for the first time—Uncle Joe's thoughts took the conversation down untraveled roads, and he spilled about his altercation with his brothers. He assumed much of the blame, something I'd never before heard him do to anyone, and confessed how much he missed them, that he didn't even have their phone numbers and had never seen many of his nieces and nephews, and now his grand-nieces and grand-nephews. He spoke of his first marriage, which, were it not for my sister's existence, I would never have suspected he'd had.

I knew his ex-wife, Florence, and had even worked for her one holiday season when she needed extra help at her store. I also knew that their divorce was anything but amicable, with each side carrying much of the burden for the dissolution of the marriage. But even my mother, who would shake her head with amusement and say "that woman" whenever Florence came up in conversation, conceded that my father was mostly at fault, even though she didn't meet him until well after the divorce. No matter how difficult Florence may have been—and "difficult," according to some, was euphemistic—my father couldn't refute his hand in the matter. "I just couldn't do it," he admitted. "I couldn't make it work with Florence. There was no way it could have worked between me and a woman like that."

Even numbed by wine I felt uncomfortable with the conversation and I longed for my father to shut up long enough to finish his steak, releasing me from a conversation I wanted nothing to do with and relieving the other patrons of having to listen to his drunken confessional. But I should have known well enough that my father couldn't stick to his promise, and I knew what would happen once the two-gin-and-tonic limit was breached. I even caught a neighboring table casting a look of pity, and I thought I saw one of them mouth, "Poor girl." At that moment, I would rather have endured a week of sex-ed classes with my mother than be seated in the Escoffier with my father—Honors College be damned.

As my father raised his gin and tonic, the liquid sloshing over the sides, he gazed at me intently, both imploring and defying me to understand. He'd tried to regale with stories of overcoming hardship, fighting anti-Semites, and escaping an ex-wife who, according to him, was nothing more than a two-bit adulteress. But none of his words held water. And then he tried to hook me with a line that he thought I'd confirm without the least struggle. And I balked: "That's why I chose your mother. Because she's simple."

I'd taken a lot from my father and had listened to him disparage many people—friends, teachers, even relatives—but this was a new low. My eyes burned as if they'd catch fire if I didn't let the tears flow, and it took all my willpower to stand without knocking over my chair. I threw my napkin in the middle of the table, returning the stubborn gaze that I'd earned through DNA, and became acutely aware of the pall of silence that had fallen over the dining room. My lower lip quivered as I fought the urge to spew a litany of pirate-worthy curses, but I opted for a more concise route. "Good night, Dad."

I turned on my heel and walked out of the Escoffier, my gaze straight ahead so as not to catch the eyes of those watching me exit.

* * *

Marta had remained remarkably silent throughout my storytelling, and I knew it wasn't due to the bocadillos we'd downed while waiting under the station awning. She'd listened with the interest of an old friend, someone habituated to my long-winded ramblings. Had she been unfamiliar with the term "dysfunctional family" before I arrived, she was well versed by the time our train pulled into the station that evening.

She didn't probe, and she didn't pass judgment. She simply accepted my tales as fact and allowed the information to simmer, then digested the newfound knowledge her traveling companion had gushed in an unanticipated wave of emotion. We climbed aboard the train, this time lucky enough to stake claim on an empty compartment. As tired as we were, we couldn't help but rehash the events of the previous twenty-four hours, my long-winded diatribe excepted.

As the train rattled on Madrid-bound through the darkened countryside, Marta and I swapped stories, bursting into guffaws at the most ludicrous anecdotes due to sheer exhaustion. I lay upside down on my side of the compartment, my hair brushing a floor that was home to various manner of suspicious substances. But I didn't care about hygiene at that moment. Even if my next shower came at double the price of the Pontevedra hotel, it would be worth it.

My shoes off, I subconsciously drummed my toes against the walls of the train compartment. Even over the rhythmic *clackety-clackety-clack* of the train, Marta could hear the sound.

"What the hell is that?" she asked.

I froze, still inverted. "What's what?"

Marta listened intently. "It's stopped. I thought someone was doing Morse code from the next compartment." I drummed again and Marta held up her hand. "There it is again."

When I realized I was producing the distracting sound, I burst into laughter. "I'm drumming my toes."

"You're *what?*"

I yanked off my socks to better display my hidden talent. Marta drew closer to see if the physiological oddity she was witnessing was indeed real. "What the hell...?" She got as close as her nose would allow. "You call that 'drumming your toes'?"

I gave an upside-down shrug.

"New Yorkers are crazy."

"And proud of it."

"Are you the craziest of all the states?"

"Intentionally crazy? Perhaps." I flipped right-side up on my seat. "We have access to any obsession we could ever crave, be it animal, vegetable, or musical. Whatever you desire is within walking or subway distance. But we're not, like, Wyoming crazy."

"What does it mean when you are *Wyoming*?" Her inflection on the last word told me she believed it to be a verb, causing me to burst into hysterics. Over the course of the next half hour, I managed to bastardize the language Marta had spent years perfecting in school and abroad, until finally we'd created a sentence never before spoken in English, replete with Mode-laden subtext.

Between guffaws, Marta managed to repeat our inane mantra: "If you're faithful, and you're devoted, drum your toes in Wyoming."

It seemed like hours before our chortles subsided, giving way to deep sighs and, eventually, restful slumber.

7

We awoke as our train pulled into the Madrid station. The sun still hung low, not yet strong enough to sap our energy. The capital city was our oyster, and even though I loathed shellfish, the idea of having the entire city once again spread before me recharged my exhausted cells and left me wholly awake to embrace the day.

This time, a new friend of Marta's awaited us. Sofia was tall—although still an inch or two shorter than me—and sported a trendy black bob and clothing so tight it appeared airbrushed onto her skin. Her smile was more rousing than any alarm clock, and I did my best to look as alert and perky as my latest, plastic-clad friend.

Still without a toothbrush, I convinced my two hostesses to stop at a roadside stand so I could purchase an apple, remembering the many televised after-school specials touting the forbidden fruit as "nature's toothbrush."

The fuzzy socks removed from my teeth, I soldiered on, following their lead to Sofia's apartment, the epitome of the Spanish urban abode:

long hallways, high ceilings, brightly lit rooms. Unlike the Pontevedra homes of Marta's cousins, Sofia's apartment was more characteristic of what I'd expect to see in a European film playing at the Anjelika. Of course, the one major difference was Sofia's bedroom, which was literally wallpapered with posters of Depeche Mode, including much of the ceiling. After dropping our bags off, the three of us met up with Sabina and a few new cohorts, who were camped out on the terrace outside of the band's hotel. How they knew where to find them, I didn't know.

Few of our newly formed circle spoke much English, so I did my best to listen and decode their Castilian slang. Although Marta's friends were more than patient with my restricted vocabulary, both sides soon tired of the elementary-level dialogue and I was left to sit back and take in the day, whilst the rest of them bantered about what we could expect at the concert, which Marta was more than pleased to fill them in on.

My stomach growled, but we weren't there to eat, as this hotel was far posher than the one in Pontevedra, and even a small plate would have been several times more than what I'd wished to pay. So we sipped our Coca-Colas and Oranginas, hoping that we'd catch a glimpse of a band member strolling in or out. For hours we sat there, and every so often I'd ask Marta how long we were staying, but I'd never get a definitive answer. After being cooped up on the train all night, I longed to explore Madrid, beyond the little I'd already seen my first day. I even suggested to Marta that I take a walk by myself, but when she insisted there was nothing nearby of interest, I resigned myself to rehydrating and trying to make sense of every fifth word of the rapidly unfolding conversation.

I had leaned back in the chair, my face pointed upwards in the hopes of becoming at least a few shades darker than paste, and was lost in my thoughts when I heard my name.

"Right, Jenn?" I sat up to find myself being stared down by everyone at the table. The looks on their faces made me suspect I'd been ratted out.

"Sorry, I wasn't listening."

Marta smirked, her expression a mixture of amusement and smugness. "I was just telling them how you're giving me your autographed Pontevedra ticket, because you lost mine. They all think it's only fair."

I glanced about the table, hoping to find the eyes of an ally, but even Sabina seemed convinced of my guilt. "Yeah, sure. I'll get my Madrid ticket signed tonight."

Marta returned to her conversation, satisfaction etched in all her features.

The tree-lined street of the hotel was home to many unseen birds, whose chirping produced the background track of the table's conversation, itself comprised of the incessant twittering of young women ecstatic for the evening's events. I managed to glean that we'd be clubbing after the concert and that they knew the Madrid haunts the band most preferred. The table was abuzz with planning when a hush fell over the group and all eyes turned to the door leading onto the patio.

Sabina nearly fell out of her seat when she spied Fletch approaching, and as he strolled to a nearby table, she held a hand to her chest as if to calm her breathing. We were the only party on the patio and Fletch, knowing why the gaggle of young women had chosen this particular hotel for overpriced soft drinks, honored us with a quick wave before taking a seat that faced a quieter direction.

"It's him," Sabina breathed. "Fletch, my favorite." Her reaction was similar to Marta's when Dave had sung to us at the Pontevedra concert.

Talk at the table turned to a whisper, with not-so-furtive glances cast in Fletch's direction every few moments. As I leaned in for a listen, I realized that each female was plotting how best to approach for an autograph, without looking hopelessly caddish. I was certain that Sofia, the most sophisticated-looking of the bunch, could best pull it off, and I suspected that she'd be elected to do the deed for the entire party.

But mild-mannered Sabina surprised me. While the others were still outlining their scheme, she slowly stood and walked over to Fletch's table. A few moments later, her actions had won her not only an autograph but a photo with her idol. She returned to the table with a grin wider than the Rio Manzanares.

I'd expected the others to be upset that they hadn't collected their own souvenirs, but they seemed genuinely pleased for Sabina, patting her on the back and offering congratulations. I took it that Sabina wasn't known as the most courageous of the bunch.

Our current mission accomplished, our gaggle left the hotel in search of lunch. We'd been parked at our wrought iron table for several hours, long enough that my legs ached and that walking was a welcome relief. I'd expected to be led to yet another cafetería but was both amazed and disappointed at their choice for our meal: McDonald's. Marta's dismissal of all things "made in America" had led me to believe that she'd be reluctant to step foot in the fast-food mega-chain, but when I saw how quickly she ordered, I realized she was a regular customer. I refrained from McRibbing her.

With the concert still hours away, we strolled at a leisurely—even by Spanish standards—pace to the Plaza del Toros, the bullring where the show would be held. Marta was only mildly surprised by the long queue that had already formed. "It is Madrid. Of course there are more people than in Pontevedra. But this many?" She eyeballed the line, mentally calculating where that would place us in the arena.

"We will probably be several rows from the stage." Not FFR, as we'd been in Pontevedra.

Marta asked her friends to watch our place in line while the two of us wandered over to the box office to claim our tickets. Our faces broke into wide grins as we collected the envelope: Tommy hadn't forgotten. Marta compared the comped tickets to the ones we'd already purchased. As guests of the band, we'd received special-edition tickets. While the hoi polloi had to content themselves with their generic "Admición" tickets, ours had "Invitación" written down the side, a mark that distinguished us from our lesser brethren. Marta held the two tickets up in the light, inspecting them as if there were a chance they were counterfeit.

"This is definitely special," she remarked, squinting at a small detail on our VIP tickets. "I was going to sell my original ticket, but I've changed my mind. This way I can show everyone the difference, and how we received special treatment." She tucked both of her tickets in her pants pocket—her bra must have felt slighted—then checked the envelope again. I noted the return of the familiar look of consternation as she stomped back to the window.

From several yards away, I could hear her arguing with the ticket agent—over what I didn't know. When she returned a moment later, she was red-faced with exasperation. "They forgot our backstage passes." She said this as if announcing the death of a family member. "We have to find Tommy."

We returned to our place in line, Marta's face resolutely set on maintaining her composure, but it was only a manner of minutes before she was erupting. "*¡Mira!* We have our tickets, and obviously we were invited—our tickets say 'invitation'—and the clerk *refuses* to give us our passes. The bastard! He claimed he didn't have any, the liar.

He probably sold them, *our* passes. But he will see. We will get our passes. Right, Jenn?" The group turned to look at me, but I was still amazed that I'd understood every word that had come out of Marta's mouth, especially considering the speed at which she'd been ranting.

"*Claro que sí*," I responded, and received a round of appreciative nods. It was only afterwards that I realized I'd mistranslated and, that by *we*, Marta had really meant *me*, and that her part in pass-procurement would consist purely of sticking a red-hot poker in my keister.

But at least I had a few moments of reprieve. When Sofia broke away from the others to introduce me to her friend, it wasn't the Spanish sun that made the heat rise under my collar. When Francisco ("*Franthisco!*") turned to shake my hand, I was confronted with a smoldering, dark-eyed Spaniard who epitomized the phrase "Latin lover." Even the glint of metallic braces hardly detracted from his smile. As he gave the obligatory Spanish greeting—three kisses on the cheeks—I nearly melted into a puddle right on the pavement outside the Plaza del Toros. I thought perhaps Sofia was playing Cupid, as there were obviously a few other friends that she didn't bother to introduce me to, until Francisco spoke.

"You are American?" he asked, his English clear but uncertain. "I too have an American friend visiting me." He waved to a young man in a baseball cap a few yards away. As soon as I saw Francisco's friend, I not only understood what Marta meant about the stamp on my forehead but also just how distinctive Midwesterners look.

The friend introduced himself as Andy from Ohio, and I could sense the others watching the interaction with some curiosity, as if visiting the monkey exhibit at the zoo. How do Americans interact? How many times do they kiss on the cheeks? Do they throw poo? Sofia seemed surprised at the formality of our handshake. "*¡Eres en*

España, no América!" Andy and I awkwardly pecked each other on the cheeks.

To make conversation, I told my compatriot that I went to school in the Midwest. "So do I," he replied.

"Really? I go to school in Michigan."

He raised an eyebrow. "So do I."

"I thought no one was from Michigan," Marta whispered over my shoulder, but I ignored her.

"University of Michigan, Ann Arbor."

Andy seemed as stunned as I was when he asked, "What dorm?"

A moment later I was properly introduced to my neighbor, who had lived one floor above me for eight full months without our ever having met.

"So," Marta said, as the line began to move, "the bodyguards are from Michigan, and here is a boy from your dorm. You told me no one's from Michigan. Are you sure Jenna Bond isn't being followed, perhaps by your father's friends?" She gave me a conspiratorial smile as we pushed ahead.

Our new cast of characters gabbed amongst ourselves as the sun broiled my pallid flesh. Andy's Spanish was much better than mine, so he had less trouble following along with the rapid-fire conversation. I did my best to keep up and chimed in a few times, but it took me so long to get the words out that I always felt self-conscious, especially as everyone else paused, their patient gazes like those of parents waiting for a child to pronounce a polysyllabic word. I soon gave up and dropped into the background, not wanting to further interrupt the rhythm of the conversation, especially considering the importance of the subject: Which clubs would our boys choose to party in that night?

Occasionally I'd cast a glance over at Francisco, admiring his strong profile and olive skin. He almost caught my gaze once, but I feigned an eye tic and he was none the wiser. But someone else noticed my stares.

"He doesn't have a girlfriend," Sabina whispered discreetly in English.

I could feel my face grow warmer, even though the sinking sun had now placed us in shade. "Who?" I asked. But I wasn't fooling anyone, let alone sharp-eyed Sabina.

"It's okay," she said. "I won't tell anyone. He *is* hot." And we both stared off at the Latin Adonis as the setting sun caressed his skin in ways that made us both wish we were sunbeams.

I felt a tug on my hand and turned to see Marta's wide-eyed expression just inches from my nose. "C'mon! We are going in!" she said, then pulled me forward so that I could once again perform my miraculous sprint for front-row seats.

But with the massive Madrid crowds, there was no way I could stake claim on such a choice location, especially considering how far back in line we were. The mobs ahead of me kicked up dust from the bullring floor and I choked as I blazed across the arena, tossing an unnecessary "*Lo siento*" every time I ran into a body through a powdery red cloud.

When finally the flesh in front of me gave no more, I knew I was as far as I could go. Through the swirling clouds of dust, I tried to gauge where I was in relation to the stage, then shuffled a little back to the right to be closer to where I knew Alan's drum set would be. Bodies pushed up behind me, and I felt the weight of several other sprinters careen into whoever was mashed against my back, a staccato of breath escaping my lungs with each impact.

The bullring buzzed like a hive in a sandstorm, with voices shouting to locate lost friends. "*¡Aquí! ¡Marta, aquí!*" I knew Marta would have trouble hearing me over the rest of the throng. My voice just didn't carry well in crowds, no matter how much I screamed. Tessa, of the Twelve Apostles, had dubbed it "the voice that only dogs could hear."

So I was relieved to hear a somewhat familiar male voice call my name. A moment later, a hand slipped into mine. It was Francisco. "Zhane! *Bueno, te he encontrado. ¿Vale?*" he asked.

"*Sí, gracias.*"

"*España,*" he said, circling a finger around his temple then motioning to the mayhem around us, "*es muy loca.*" He grinned, his braces flashing through the dusty fog.

"*Sí, un poquito. Pero me gusta… mucho.*" Hell, I was not only flirting, I was flirting bilingually.

The swarm behind us parted as if allowing Moses to pass. A moment later, a red-powdered Marta and her coughing mob had caught up with us.

"Not bad," Marta said, assessing our position. "Not bad at all. I see you've chosen Alan's side of the stage. He's her favorite," she informed the rest of our collective. The women nodded knowingly, while Francisco and Andy rolled eyeballs.

But my work wasn't over. "Okay, we need the passes. Jenn, do you see Bryan?" I popped onto my tiptoes to peer over the crowd in front of me, but no luck. "Okay, we'll have to think of something else." Marta's gestures were as grandly elaborate as if she weren't sardined by ten thousand other fans, and each time she moved she bumped someone around her.

She was unmindful—or, more likely, uncaring—of their caustic glares every time she inadvertently elbowed them in the ribs, shoulder, or jaw. She looked back towards the entrance and spied the control board in the center of the arena floor. There, speaking with the light technician, was a familiar face. "Jenn, there's Jimmy! He'll help us. *¡Vaya!*" She gave a light shove that propelled me no further than Francisco's foot, and he stifled a yelp. But a second later, after Marta had waved her arm frantically over the neighboring crowds, the red-dusted sea parted for me and I was able to slip past the sweaty, dirt-covered bodies towards the control booth.

Jimmy flashed a broad smile. "Señorita Footie, how's it going?"

I told him our predicament, and Jimmy suggested exiting the stadium to search for Ron the Swagman, the keeper of backstage passes. I wished Jimmy good luck on his set and continued on my latest quest. After talking a Spanish security guard into readmitting me once I'd left the stadium, I left the dust cloud of the bullring and reentered the plaza, which was now so empty it seemed as if an apocalypse had since taken place.

The sun outside the bullring seemed to shine even brighter than inside, where I'd felt as if my pasty skin had been on slow-bake. Marta had told me that my vampirish complexion was an insult to the Iberian Peninsula's famed rays. I reminded her that the schedule we were keeping had been her idea and that I hadn't planned to travel across the entire country without seeing more than three hours of natural light. She'd shrugged off my words with the declaration that nocturnal living was well worth the ecstatic high she was now feeling.

After nearly an hour of being directed from one pass-less body-guard to the next pass-less roadie, I found Ron the Swagman, who was on guard just outside the Plaza de Toros.

The Swagman was easy to identify amid the Spanish crowds outside the bullring. His pale skin, ginger hair, and distinct, self-important strut made him stick out like a goth at a pep rally. "Are you the Swagman?" I asked with confidence, certain by now he'd been radioed that I was on my way and that the whole transaction only required a few pleasantries before I rejoined the throngs inside.

His blue eyes glinted as he exhaled a cloud of smoke. "Might be. Depends what you're after." Something about the Swagman's demeanor made me stop a few feet further than I normally would have, and I reverted to a mode usually reserved for interacting with drunkards on the subway.

"Jimmy said I should come see you, said you'd have some passes for me and my friends." I couldn't put a finger on the source of my unease, but my gut told me to keep my distance.

The Swagman sneered. "Jimmy who?" The question caught me off guard. Surely he knew the members of the opening band. When I told the Swagman that I meant Jimmy from Marxman, his sneer grew more pronounced. "I don't answer to him," he spat. I tried to place his accent, but the best I could do was label it as decidedly un-English. Irish? Scottish? Welsh? "But I can get you passes, if you want 'em."

My spirits leapt. Jimmy hadn't led me astray after all. "Of course! Sure! Thank you, Sw—er, Ron."

As the Swagman's gaze narrowed and he took a step closer, a chill ran down my sweat-soaked spine. "You know what you have to do then, right?" The meaning of his words was clear and my heart fell into my stomach. My eyes must have widened in shock because the Swagman laughed at my reaction. I decided that my best defense was to play naive.

"Uh, no. I've never had to *do* anything for passes before." I hoped that these words would make him realize I wasn't like those other fans, that I wasn't one to stoop to such self-deprecating acts for a few paltry pieces of adhesive-backed paper, that I was special and deserved the preferential treatment to which I'd recently become accustomed. I stood rooted to the spot, watching him posture and drag on his cigarette as if he hadn't heard me.

When he stopped and exhaled, he didn't even appear to be speaking to me when his lips moved. His eyes remained narrowed and focused on some object in the distance. "You know what you have to do," he murmured.

I tried appealing to our commonalities. "Come on," I cajoled, "do a fellow redhead a favor." He didn't so much as turn. The Swagman stood in silhouette to me, his head tilted slightly back, smoke streaming lazily from his nostrils. "A fellow redhead *and* Irish kin."

I'd struck a chord. The Swagman was turning. "I'm Scottish." His lip curled with the same derision mine would have if someone had called me a Jersey girl. His gaze locked with mine, then his eyes traveled down to my knees and back up again. "You're a smart girl, with some semblance of intelligence." His snarl eased a bit, and I thought he might actually be on the verge of cracking a smile. "The transaction is really quite simple."

I sighed as if he had won, but I was only trying to stretch the game further. "Right. Just like New York." As I began digging in my pockets, I could feel the Swagman's eyes looking me over and I fought hard to repress a look of repulsion. "Look, I have $100 dollars—American. That should be more than enough for two backstage passes." I held the money out towards him with a broad, almost coquettish smile on my face. I would be nothing if not amenable, in spite of the circumstances.

But the Swagman scoffed at my offer. "You think I want that?" He turned and exhaled a large gray plume. "I'm loaded. What would I want with your money?" He shook his head as if scorning my ignorance, his clear eyes set in the middle of a reddened face that might have been attractive if not for the malevolence it held. "You're from New York, you say? Then you're not some dumb babe-in-the-woods."

I knew then that the Swagman was not willing to barter with me, that there was only one way I'd get those passes. He drew nearer, as if sensing my reluctance, but I didn't budge, although he was mere inches away. Even when he blew a waft of smoke in my face, I hardly blinked. When he next started to speak, I felt a piece of me awaken that I hadn't known existed.

"I don't want your money, dearie." He made a sweeping gesture around the near-empty plaza, eyeing the remaining teenage girls as he did so. "I can have any beautiful Spanish girl I want with those passes." He took a step closer as he let the words to set in. The smell of sweat and smoke was overwhelming, and I fought back the bile in my throat. "And when I come to New York, I'll be able to have any beautiful American girl as well." His eyes glared with triumph as he took another drag of his cigarette, but I stepped back before he had a chance to exhale again.

A mixture of pure anger, loathing, and hatred welled up inside my chest as my breath came in short bursts through my nostrils, the commonality of his red hair enraging me even further. It wasn't just that he was spoiling my adventure. His cocky swagger and self-important smugness were like a smack in the face. He was a pathetic specimen of a human being, one who used his menial position just to get a piece of ass, and for that I almost pitied him. But then I thought of all the young women he'd most likely taken advantage of over the years, all the desperate, timid females he'd "bartered" with.

It was then that I recalled the words my father had told me long ago, words I'd dismissed because I never dared believe I'd ever have reason to use them. But there they were, bubbling up from the recesses of my memory to remind me that I was not powerless, even if that power lay outside of myself.

"If anyone ever hurts you," my father had said, his eyes blazing from gin and tonics, "you come to *me.*" He stabbed his finger pointedly in his chest. "You come to me," he continued, "and I'll make them disappear"—he snapped his fingers—"like that."

Perhaps I'd dismissed my father's words not because I hadn't believed in the power he claimed to wield but because I couldn't conceive of a situation in which I'd ever need such drastic measures. The furthest I'd ever used my father's limited notoriety was to treat my friends to the occasional pu-pu platter. But meeting the Swagman had recalled that memory for a reason.

I shot the iciest stare I could manage at the Swagman, who, by his expression, seemed to mistake me as a victim resigned to her fate. He stamped out his cigarette and assumed a stance that was just short of pulling down his zipper. I almost smiled when I thought about what would have happened to him had our exchange occurred on the other side of the Atlantic. The image pleased me. "I'll see you in America then." My voice was unnervingly steady and his cocky grin faded to bewilderment as I spoke my parting words. "I'll be sure you receive the New York welcome you deserve."

Before he had a chance to respond, I turned and headed back into the bullring, my head brimming with pictures of cement shoes dragging the Swagman to the floor of the Hudson.

I pressed back through the crowd and somehow managed to find my posse, and poise. Marta could tell by the look on my face that my quest had been fruitless.

"*¿Que pasó?*" she asked. "You look upset."

"I didn't get the passes." I avoided her glance. I didn't want to go into details just then.

"I can tell that. But what happened?"

"Can we talk about this later?"

She looked as if she might press further but didn't. "Sure, *claro*."

We remained standing for at least another two hours, banal chatter filling the time. Francisco and Andy had allowed the womenfolk to stand in front and so took the brunt of the shoving from the mob behind us. As the heat rose to levels just below stir-fry, I could feel the sweat tracing lines through the dust on my skin.

I spotted Bryan working the front of the stage and borrowed a pen from Sofia. On a scrap of paper I wrote a hasty note to Tommy, explaining briefly what had transpired with the Swagman. Somehow I managed to pass the note to Bryan, and he obliged by promising to deliver it.

When the rosy glow of evening announced that the temperature would finally begin to fall, I breathed easy, knowing that once the bands took the stage I would forget all unpleasantries and once again be transported to that otherworldly place where time stood still and nothing else mattered.

Marxman came on while there was still some light in the sky, and their show was on par with the one in Pontevedra, the crowd reacting similarly to their Columbus number but seeming to enjoy the rest of the set, or at least tolerating it. After all, it was their idols who had chosen the opening act, so the band must've had *some* merit.

But the intermission between sets was even longer than that in Pontevedra, and because there was little wind in the city, we didn't have to worry about the curtains causing problems with the equipment as at the previous concert. I spotted Tommy at the control booth and once more wedged my way through the crowd. I didn't go into details, but I let Tommy know that his foosball partner had been treated less than kindly. He told me he'd talk with the Swagman, but I couldn't tell from his demeanor exactly how the conversation would unfold. After seeing him fume and want to toss el stalkero off a bridge, he hardly seemed to care about this latest incident. I shrugged it off. The Swagman would be in New York soon enough.

Reunited with my clique, I allowed myself to relax, content that I was about to experience another concert, which was the whole point of my coming to Spain in the first place. All my worries dissolved when the lights finally dimmed and the familiar opening notes boomed throughout the bullring. This time, the opening number went off without a hitch. The curtains fell as planned, the music was as clear as a Galician summer day, and the crowd, as if partaking in a religious ceremony, stopped shoving and became one with the universe—or, at least, the arena.

Without a front-row position, we didn't have the advantage of watching every move of our favorite band members and instead had to dodge and weave our heads at the whim of whoever stood in front of us. But even more so than in Pontevedra, the Madrid crowd celebrated the music, singing along as if to hymns. When the opening chords to "Stripped" reverberated over our heads, the arena reacted by holding up a multitude of lighters, the likes of which hadn't been seen since Lynyrd Skynyrd's 1973 Cow Palace concert. Without a roof over our heads, the stars shone brilliantly down onto the *madrileños*, forming a seamless tapestry of glittering lighters and celestial orbs.

I spent much time glancing about, taking in the various unknown faces as they sang enchanted, seemingly unmindful that the lyrics were in a foreign tongue. Even those with perfect views of the band had their eyes shut tightly, in a near religious rapture similar to what I imagined Marta and her step-carrying brothers felt each Easter.

Perhaps it was the myriad bodies pressing upon me, or the pure elation of the independence of being on another continent, or the euphoria of experiencing simultaneously the emotions of those around me, but whatever it was, I couldn't recall a previous moment where I'd felt so at peace, so happy to be alive. During "Judas," a fine enough song, although not quite as grand as other tracks from *Songs of Faith and Devotion*, the lyrics took on new meaning, as if written by a higher power. For someone as faithless as myself—who had joined Bible school in first grade because I liked Bobby Strider's haircut and had since declared all religion anathema to the point of infuriating both spiritually challenged parents—the concert meant more to me than any church or synagogue service, and I knew this even with my limited attendance at either. At long last, I was one of the devout.

The concert over, the stadium began to empty, but our little group remained huddled near the stage, awaiting word from me or Marta about what to do regarding backstage passes. While we conferred about our next steps, Marta groused about the girl Dave had pulled on stage. "He *never* does that *ever.*" I half expected her to throw a tantrum in the middle of the bullring. "Why couldn't he have done that in Pontevedra when I was in the front row? What's *wrong* with him?" Sofia threw a consoling arm around her, as upset with Dave as her friend was.

Within a few moments, it was clear that backstage guests were not being let through via the front of the stage, as they had been in Pontevedra, and so we begrudgingly left the Plaza del Toros, taking our time in doing so. Once outside, Marta perked up again, her radar on backstage-pass alert. "There," she said, pointing towards a side entrance.

I spotted the location where guests were waltzing in, their stickered clothing gaining them admittance to the most exclusive of locales. Our black-clad posse parked itself just yards away from the security guards, none of who had American billboards on their foreheads. "They're locals," Marta said with disgust. "They'll never let us in."

Sabina hadn't said a word since we'd left the stadium and, as I scanned her face, I suspected she was the most anxious of all of us to gain access. She retained an aura of hope, her eyes shining every time she heard an English-speaking voice.

"This is ridiculous," Marta objected. "Tommy told us we'd have passes. That window clerk... if I could see him now." She clenched a threatening fist. I didn't doubt her conviction to pummel a minimum-wage earner who'd prevented her from attaining any goal, no matter how prosaic.

We stood there for half an hour, our hopes dwindling by the minute. Every time a group exited, each of us would cast an endearing gaze in their direction, hoping they'd somehow take pity and help us gain admittance.

"There's still the clubs," Sofia said, her optimism as resilient as ever. "We'll see them there, definitely."

But there was a certain cachet in gaining backstage access that none of us wanted to give up on. A stickered pass emblazoned on your chest signified you were of importance, not some fly-by-night simpleton who owned "all three of the band's albums," but a hardcore Devotee deserving of tête-à-tête interaction. A pass conferred not just admittance but acceptance.

Our faith wavering, we prepared to leave and head to the first of the clubs where, should the gods favor us, we'd encounter the band. Just as we were about to concede failure, a high-heeled cognoscenti tramped out past security, her perfectly coiffed hair bouncing in rhythm to her stride. As she passed mere inches from me, the high priestess of partying slapped two passes on my thigh. "Act discreet," she murmured without making eye contact, as inconspicuous as a well-trained spy. Her American accent made me wonder if I was as obvious as Marta claimed. She didn't break stride as she sauntered off to catch up with her entourage, not even so much as casting a backwards glance.

Before the clacking of her heels had faded, Marta had ripped the second pass from my skin. "You did it! I knew you would!" She was positively triumphant as I tried to calm her down, afraid the security guards would notice and suspect we had second-hand clearance. Francisco, whom moments earlier I'd noticed inching towards me, faded into the background. "Well." Marta glanced about at our group, unable to suppress her grin. "I guess we'll meet you back here in an hour or two?"

Sabina's face puckered as if she might burst into tears. Although I felt like the most wretched of human beings, I couldn't bring myself to sacrifice my pass to her. Even if I'd wanted to, I doubt Marta would have let her foosball-champion friend stay behind.

With confidence leading her, Marta strode past security, her stickered chest thrust forward. I followed closely behind, imparting frequent *perdones* as I brushed past those who truly belonged back-stage. We soon found ourselves in a much more lavish set-up than that in Pontevedra, the big city being more accustomed to catering to elite guests.

Within moments, Tommy had spotted us and waved a hirsute arm to join him in a foosball game. With only one spot open, I gladly filled in opposite our wild-eyed friend, partnering with Hollis, Marxman's lead singer. Tommy and his Spanish teammate beat us soundly, reminding me that I'd do well to spend less time in the stacks and more time at whichever frat had the most level table. I blamed my poor playing on Alan, whom I spied watching our tournament from a few feet away. Without even looking up from the game, I could feel the weight of his stare, and I imagined it was directed at me and not the table as a whole.

Tommy celebrated his victory the way he celebrated most every event—with a beer—while Marta went in search of Dave, leaving me momentarily alone with the bassist. When we had as much privacy as could be hoped for, given the surrounding party atmosphere, I took a gamble. "So, I see you have a new drummer."

Half of Tommy's beer was gone with the first sip. "Yeah, we were lucky with that. Our tour manager pulled a few favors with friends. Worked out alright, suppose." His expression gave me no hint as to whether or not he held me responsible for the fire-drill job search.

"All right, there you are." Jimmy of the emerald-green eyes beamed in our direction. "We're heading over to the next party, mate."

Although he'd been speaking to his bandmate, I took the opportunity to thank Jimmy for his help earlier and apologized for bothering him. In his typical light-hearted manner, he simply smiled and said, "Okay," a light nod concluding the conversation. "Meet you there, mate." He slapped Tommy on the shoulder in farewell.

"Pub crawl before the club?" I ventured.

Tommy cracked another beer. "Nah." With a single gulp, another half a bottle had disappeared. "Ain't feeling so well. I was up puking all last night after being out with me boys. Think I'll just stay in the hotel tonight. Get some rest." I felt my stomach sink. Without Tommy, we'd have virtually no guarantee we'd even get in, let alone receive the proper introductions we'd hoped for. "You go on though. The boys know ye. You'll have no problem getting in the VIP. As a matter of fact, this girlie here could help ye." Tommy put out an enormous paw to stop a petite blonde, the very same one who'd nearly received a Pontevedra pummeling from Marta.

Upon seeing me, the blonde appeared somewhat frightened, as if mentally connecting Marta's leering to me. I wanted no ill blood between me and anyone associated with my newfound friends and so decided to staunch whatever hostility, real or imaginary, existed between us. I thrust a hand in her direction and made sure my smile was Pollyanna friendly. "Nice to meet you. I'm Jenna."

After seeming to flinch at my movement, the blonde gripped my hand, her tiny one firmly upon mine, and began the obligatory European greeting of kissing multiple cheeks. "Christiane," she said, her voice so soft it was nearly swept away in the buzz of the party. Although she had an English lilt, there was a distinct tinge of another accent, which I guessed to be French. She was not, however, Marta's Gallic arch-nemesis, Adrienne.

"Tommy says he's not coming out tonight," I informed her, elbowing the bassist playfully in the ribs. "Can you believe that?"

"Oh no," she demurred. "The Madrid clubs are wonderful. He must come."

For the next several minutes, we tried unsuccessfully to change Tommy's mind, but there was no budging the hung-over Irishman, despite how much he seemed to enjoy the fawning of two females.

I wanted Tommy to join us not simply because he could aid Marta and me in our mission, but also because I enjoyed speaking with him, especially about music. My technical knowledge was limited by lack of ability with any instrument more difficult than a kazoo, and so I enjoyed getting Tommy's professional perspective. He could explain how sounds were achieved, why a particular chord change was so difficult, and speculated who among the latest crop of new artists he thought would be around for the long haul.

Christiane was a wealth of information, which I supposed she'd gleaned from other band members, and with little effort I managed to plot our course for the night. No sooner had she bid me and Tommy *adieu* then Marta was by my side, her face scarcely hiding her irritation at my new sidekick. Before Tommy left for his hotel, she had me ask him for passes in Barcelona. "Remind him what happened this past time," she coached. "We don't want another confrontation with the Swagman." I noted her use of "we" and almost asked her where the hell she was while the redheaded bastard was accosting me but decided that it was best to present a united front. Tommy assured us that this time, the tickets—and passes—would be waiting at will-call.

An hour later, reunited outside with our entourage, Marta and I relayed our backstage tale to a captive audience intent on hearing every last detail. By the time our cab arrived at the club Archy, our listeners were asking so many questions we'd hardly made it through retelling the foosball game. "What was Martin drinking?" Everything in sight. "Was Alan still wearing his leather pants?" Oh God, yes. "What was Dave like?" Marta's response to Sofia's question was shaded with frustration and disappointment.

"He wasn't even there! Again!" She appeared to be taking his absence personally, as if he'd stood her up. "The other three were all there. But where was Dave? *Why not Dave?*"

Archy did not have the security we'd expected. The enormous nightclub, which spanned two floors and had several bars conveniently located throughout, was packed to the rafters with chic *madrileños* swaying to electronic beats. In my white cut-offs and clingy burgundy bodysuit (which I'd rinsed out in our Pontevedra hotel room), I felt severely underdressed, especially next to Sofia, who was decked out in a black patent-leather outfit so shiny I could have used it to check the application of my lipstick. At least Marta was clad in her concert t-shirt, which, although apropos, was considerably more casual. My only fear was that my garb made me even more blatantly American. During my four days in Spain, I hadn't noticed a single European wearing cut-offs.

Back in Manhattan, I'd frequented bars quite often, downtown establishments not being terribly strict with their carding; for those that were, I simply flashed the driver's license borrowed from Ilene, my sister who had also gifted me with a free apartment on the Upper West Side. In the weeks before my trip, I'd become a regular at Terra Blues, a second-floor hole-in-the-wall on Bleecker Street, but I'd also made a point of hitting several concerts at Roseland, The Ritz, and Limelight, some of the city's most lauded music clubs. The code of the Twelve Apostles all but forbade me from stepping foot in a venue frequented by the bridge-and-tunnel contingent, so I'd never witnessed the gauche opulence common to such venues.

Archy represented all that extravagance and more, a grand-scale nightlife complex intent on providing its jet-setting clientele with the best vices Madrid had to offer. As the lighting system swept the dance floor, providing fleeting snapshots of the well-heeled patrons grinding with their partners, I imagined that New York's Studio 54 in its heyday probably looked quite similar.

Our posse had dwindled down to the diehards among us, which turned out to be only the womenfolk. I was slightly disappointed not to see *Franthisco*, but Marta and I were leaving the next day for *Barthelona*, so it wasn't as if I could have expected anything meaningful to have transpired. And besides, the ultimate object of my affections was shrink-wrapped in black leather somewhere nearby, perhaps only feet from where I stood. This was not the time for distractions.

In the course of the cab ride across town, I had unknowingly been made head of our scouting party, and as we made our entrance into the main room, Marta nudged me forward. "Do you see Bryan? Or Jimmy? Or Hollis?" Her eyes scanned the throng flickering under the throbbing club lights. "I hope they are not in the VIP room. We'll never get in there."

I'd been going to nightclubs since I was 14 and—although the ones I frequented then were of the cheesy, underage, Long Island variety—now considered myself a veteran of the club scene, despite not yet being of legal age. These teen venues had merely been warm-ups, and soon I'd graduated to The Angle, a new-wave haven for the regrettably under-twenty-one crowd, where the Twelve Apostles and I found ourselves every Saturday, and thereafter every Friday after the opening of Hotel Leningrad, an industrial spin-off.

The Angle, and all of its Long Island derivatives, was where I shed the cocoon foisted upon me by high school conformity. This underage club is, in fact, where I originally met almost every one of the Twelve Apostles, who soon became my high school clique outside of my de facto high school. The Apostles came from all strata of the Island—North Shore Catholic schools, South Shore public schools, mid-island generic suburbia. Despite our differences in socio-economic background, we forged a foundation based on the commonality of music, a foundation that proved far stronger than all the years I'd spent with classmates who understood so little about me that they'd labeled me more than just a nerd, but a *freak* nerd, a label that is hard to overcome in even the best of John Hughes scenarios.

After nearly a decade of awkward social stumbling through the pep assemblies, sports teams, and honors programs at my high school, I'd found a home to call my own.

One of the Apostles, Don, was now a Manhattan DJ, and I spent practically every weekend at The Bank as a VIP of my high school comrade-in-arms. Even when I knew no one inside, I somehow managed to talk my way past security at practically any nightclub, my underage status only aiding my mission, and often procured special treatment. It was the closest thing to a superpower I could claim.

I surveyed the landscape and felt wholly renewed. This was my element—if just a tad more brazen than usual—and Marta's encouragement to lead the group only made me more self-assured. I knew that poise was of the utmost importance, that behaving as if you belonged meant more than any self-adhesive pass ever could. A quick head motion signaled to my followers that we should surge forward.

As a collective group, we strode past the first of many bars then made our entrance into the main room, where the upper dance floor afforded the perfect view to size up the competition. None of the usual suspects were present—no one from Depeche, Marxman, not even a roadie—which could mean only one thing.

"There must be a VIP room," I told Marta. "We're going to have to find Bryan or Christiane. And let me know if you see anyone who looks like they're from Detroit." She cast me a perplexed stare. "It's in Michigan." When I'd received my acceptance to the University of Michigan, I'd never expected the prestige of the school to be outweighed by such seemingly inconsequential connections as those I'd made with the band's bodyguards.

"There he is!" From our vantage point on the stairs above the dance floor, Marta spotted Martin, who stood out among the other clubbers due to both his singular dance style and the adorable flop-piness of his bleached-blonde hair, which bounced and changed Technicolor hues under the club lighting. Even from the other side of the cavernous room, his inebriation was evident. Not far from him stood Fletch, who was prudent enough to use a nearby bar to aid him in remaining upright.

"Are we really here?" Sabina asked, her brown eyes growing larger as she took in every aspect of her surroundings. "That's really Martin? I'm not dreaming?"

Sofia threw her arms around her shorter friend. "It's real," she told her. "That's really him." The two of them stood next to each other, their arms entwined, staring out at the dance floor like anthropologists discovering a long-lost society.

We assumed a place on the floor only yards away from Martin and proceeded to dance as if we weren't surrounded by synth-god royalty. We moved as a collective unit, each of us glancing over in his direction every so often, pretending he was no one of importance, even though our lives held more meaning because of his torment-ridden songwriting.

Finally, even the indefatigable Martin needed a breather and withdrew to a comfy seat that afforded him a view of the dance floor. "I'm going to speak to him," Sofia said, adjusting her patent-leather outfit in preparation. But before she had taken a step forward, a long-legged vixen claimed the adjacent seat, throwing her legs over the floppy-haired lyricist as if locking him in. Sofia bristled. "How *dare* she!" As she threw out a few select epithets, I did my best to catalogue them in my ever-growing Spanish glossary. Sofia looked on, certain that her favorite band member was being held against his will. "He can't possibly find her attractive!" she declared before stomping over to a nearby bar to find solace in a mixed drink. I followed, liquid courage being essential to overcoming the shyness that would prevent me from engaging in a one-on-one conversation with Alan.

And then I spotted him—and her. In a dark recess just beyond the bar, the dark-haired object of my affections sat with a longhaired coquette, who pawed at every crevice of his body as if they were in their own private boudoir. Although Alan barely moved and didn't return the petting, he obviously didn't mind the attention, and my face flushed to think of what it would be like to be in her place, even though I abhorred public displays of affection and had scarcely thought of Alan in that way before arriving in Spain. When he lifted his gaze to peer about, I turned quickly away and focused my sights on reaching the bar.

"Tequila sunrise," I said to the bartender, but he only shrugged, shaking his head to demonstrate that the name of my drink did not have international renown. I required something stronger than a beer and couldn't think how to translate any of the drinks I knew. Ordering libations had been conveniently omitted from my Spanish textbooks. *"Una margarita?"* I took his reply to mean that he didn't have a blender. *"Vale, una bebida muy fuerte, con mucha fruta."* That seemed to do the trick.

I returned to our coffee klatch, fruity concoction in hand and proud that I'd once again managed to order on my own, even if the drink did cost more than my train ride from Pontevedra. "Any sign of your quarry?" I asked Marta.

"None." She slapped her hands on her sides, miffed that she'd once again been stood up. "What the hell is he doing? What's more important than being *here*?"

"Maybe he's found someone to hole up with, like Alan did." I motioned with my drink to where Alan and the skank sat.

"Oh no!" Marta grabbed my hand, shaking her head as if I'd been betrayed. "That should be you, not some... some... chipper!"

I stifled my amusement, not wanting to offend Marta while she was backing my cause. "It's okay, I wouldn't want to be her anyway."

"No?" Marta looked as if she'd just learned the Pope wore frilly lingerie. "But that is your man. You wouldn't want to touch him like she does?" Her frantic hand gestures were enough to make me almost spew my fruity *bebida* out my nose.

"I'd rather have my dignity, thank you."

"Screw dignity," Marta snorted. Her green eyes took on a faraway stare as if reliving a favorite fantasy. "What I wouldn't give to touch Dave and his—"

"It's him! It's him!" Sabina barged in on our conversation and gestured wildly at the balcony above us. We raised our heads to spy the longhaired silhouette that had been evading us since our journey began. A soft gasp escaped Marta's lips.

"Dave."

Her reverence for the lead singer was almost as great as the pride in her country. She gazed heavenwards as if accepting the body of Christ, emerald eyes seeking out the face that was obscured by shadows. Without even glancing in her direction, I could feel her tension and anticipated her next words.

"Jenn, take me up there."

"But I don't—"

"*Take me.*"

There's no arguing with obsession. But before I could act, we all watched as Dave turned and disappeared toward the staircase to the main floor. Marta gripped my shoulder so that my arm lost feeling. "He's coming," she breathed, her repeated words barely audible above the thumping bass. "He's *coming*."

Moments later, the most elusive of band members was walking but steps away from our entourage, his stride purposeful, his poise as cocksure as ever, and his hand clenching a half-finished magnum of top-shelf champagne. His swagger was a mix of arrogance and inebriation, and as he took his place in the center of the dance floor, all eyes fell upon him.

From the murmuring about me, I could tell that some of the other patrons had no clue about the identity of the scraggly, over-tattooed skeleton who somehow commanded so much attention. But as Dave began dancing, a respectful circle formed about him, his admirers allowing him the spotlight he so craved while the uninitiated reacted to the cognoscenti that did as they were bid.

I felt a piece of paper get shoved into my hand and looked down to find a ticket from the Madrid show. "Get his autograph for me, Jenn." Marta's eyes glowed from within the shadows that concealed her face. Every now and again, a light illuminated her intensity. "You promised me you would."

The crowd had tightened the circle around the man of the hour, and I scanned the many faces eager to take that extra step further in. "Not now," I said. "This isn't the time."

"But you *will*." It was more of a statement of fact than a plea. "You *will* get it for me."

I hadn't yet drunk enough to be so easily persuaded into promising anything. "I'll try, if there's a chance."

"There's a chance *now*," she implored. "There's no one around, he's practically alone..."

Her voice trailed off as a svelte, dark-skinned Amazon broke through the circle and sidled up to Marta's would-be paramour. As the two began an immodest tango that rivaled mating rituals documented by National Geographic, I could feel the heat of Marta's rage boiling beneath her skin. After only a few moments of such display, she'd had her fill and retreated to the bar. I ordered another fruity tonic, my head barely beginning to feel the effects of the first.

While Marta and I consoled ourselves with high-octane beverages, Christiane appeared at my side. "There you are," she said as if we'd been acquaintances longer than three hours. With her back to Marta, she was oblivious to the icy glares my Spanish host threw in her direction. I still hadn't filled Marta in on Christiane's non-Adrienne identity. "This is not a bad club, *non?*" Her clear eyes scanned the room, taking in both the spectacle of Dave with his skank du jour and the fashionistas who were as much a part of the ambience as the lighting and smoke effects.

The flamboyance of Archy was as unfamiliar to me as if I'd happened into the Spanish palace itself. The most noteworthy extravagance of my favorite Manhattan bars, including The Bank where Don DJ'd, was the use of gallons of matte black paint as the predominant basis of decor. Had I the continental experience of my European comrades, I wouldn't have had to worry about such trivial matters as the difference between being 18 and 21, and by now would have been well versed in the ways of gaudy and glitzy nightclubs.

"It's okay," I conceded, hoping my inexperience wasn't overly blatant. "A little ostentatious, but it's fun."

I sensed Marta wedging herself closer to me and my newly minted French colleague and decided it was time to make proper introductions.

"Marta, this is *Christiane*." I exaggerated the pronunciation, leaving no chance for misunderstanding. "Christiane, this is Marta."

They exchanged European pleasantries—*kiss kiss*—and I could tell that any animosity Marta had been feeling toward Christiane had greatly subsided, now that identity was no longer a mystery. Christiane all but ignored Marta's presence after their introduction.

"I have not seen Bryan all evening," Christiane said in a demure voice that was almost washed away by the techno-racket blaring from the speakers. "Do you know where I can find him?" I was more than amused that Marta should witness an insider probing me for such privileged answers.

"No, but Alan's over in the corner. Bryan can't be far away."

Christiane's face remained as consistently indifferent as that of a Botox patient, and I realized I'd yet to see her so much as smile or sneer. "Perhaps," she said, her lips pursing in that particular way of the French, as if kissing her words *adieu*. "I shall go find him. *A bientôt*."

Although my second encounter with the French Moder was even briefer than the first, it served to remind Marta that I was not wholly alone in our adventure. "She does not seem bad… for a Frenchie," she conceded.

"She's rather nice. At least, Tommy seems to think so." I was already halfway through my latest drink and seriously contemplating another.

"Had she been Adrienne," Marta started, as I knew she would, "I would not have been so polite."

I didn't make eye contact as I stirred my drink. "I know."

"But Christiane seems okay," she repeated awkwardly, perhaps realizing for once the absurdity of her voiced inadequacies. "It's 'Christiane,' isn't it?"

"Mm-hmm." I was enjoying Marta's discomfort. The tables had turned, and I was in the enviable position of knowing more insiders than my host. If she was to get any closer to the band, Marta knew she would need me.

But before she had the chance to pester me again for Dave's autograph, Sofia brought us news that the band was headed to the next leg of the party. "We're off to Pacha," she announced, beckoning us with the wag of a slender finger.

After I'd downed the remainder of my drink, our posse crammed into the back of a taxi, its red-striped door making it appear more like an emergency vehicle than a mundane mode of transport. Moments later, we'd arrived at our next stop, a nightclub even more extravagant than the first. Although I had no idea what "Pacha" meant—it could have been a disease for all I knew—the interior was appropriately posh, the clientele even more affluent than at Archy. As a collective black mass, we sauntered inside as if we held the deed to the joint.

"You know," Marta said, making chitchat as we waited for our drinks at the bar, "when we were all dancing together, right before Dave came downstairs, Alan was watching all of us." I tried not to appear too interested. After all, it was the music that had brought me to another continent, not the thought of some pasty Brit's ass wrapped in black leather. It was Marta who was hopelessly obsessed, Marta who made embarrassing squeezing gestures at Dave so that all of Pontevedra could see, Marta who betrayed her thoughts by licking her lips as her eyes rolled heavenwards deep in lustful thought. I was rational, not some rabidly fanatical American who would jump into bed with a guy simply because he was a rock god. Marta should have learned that by now.

"All of us?" I tossed the bartender a few pesetas then leaned against the bar rail. "I'm sure if he was ogling anyone, it was Sofia."

"He had a wandering eye," Marta assured me. "Of course he looked at Sofia, but he couldn't be satisfied with just one. And"—she moved in closer as if about to pass me top-secret CIA documents—"I noticed he wasn't wearing his wedding ring. Do you suppose Jeri knows?"

I could only assume that Jeri was Alan's wife. I hadn't bothered to memorize trivial information such as band birthdays or family trees. What mattered to me was his musical prowess, the way his compositions brought depth to the band's repertoire (as evidenced by the difference between the colorless second album, *A Broken Frame,* and the more emotive *Construction Time Again,* produced when Alan had become a full-fledged band member, even writing some of the tracks), and how deep his passion for music ran (multiple viewings of *101* had taught me that). His sculpted muscles, the way he threw himself into his drums, the soft glisten of sweat while performing under the harsh concert lights—all that I'd only recently come to confess an appreciation to. An absent wedding ring only added to the allure.

Not that I'd ever have the balls to do anything about it. I'd harbored long-term infatuations on mortals for years without so much as admitting it to a soul, much less approach the object of my affection about it. There was no way I'd ever be able to muster the courage to strike up a conversation with Alan on my own, let alone attempt to seduce someone of his stature, a man desired by a multitude of women—and some men. What chance did I, a blatantly American nobody, have against these Amazons and long-legged flirts?

When Marta took off in search of Dave, Sabina claimed her spot at the bar. We chatted amiably, and she seemed appreciative of my time, as if my limited encounters with the band had somehow elevated my status just slightly above that of the rest of our entourage. As we were thick in a debate over the virtues of Erasure versus Yaz, Sabina spotted Dave entering the main hall then quickly disappearing up a flight of stairs guarded by a pair of American simians.

"We'll never get up there," Sabina lamented, and I recalled the look on her face when Marta and I strolled backstage, leaving her in the dust of the bullring.

The liquid courage burned through my veins a little stronger than before and, after ordering one more drink to maintain the perfect buzz, I pulled Sabina aside. "There's more than one way into a room," I whispered, and pointed to the stairs. "That's the VIP entrance, but look." We peered at the level above, where a few select faces mingled and gazed down on the hoi polloi. "You see? Servers. *Camareros.* They have to get up there somehow too, and they're not using the same entrance as the band. I guarantee that."

The sparkle in Sabina's eyes came from within, not from the myriad spinning house lights that would have caused seizures in an epileptic. "You think we can find it?" Sabina must've thought I was either a private dick or a descendant of Sir Arthur Conan Doyle. "How do you know all this?"

"I've worked in food service the past five years. Never in a million years did I think that catering bat mitzvahs would help me crash a rock-star party."

Moments later, Sabina and I found ourselves at the bottom of a well-lighted flight of stairs. "This is it," I told her. "It's not as dark so the servers can see when they're carrying trays. Plus it's not carpeted. Makes it easier to clean up spills."

We slid back into the shadows as a bartender came tramping down the steps with a tray full of dirty glasses. He breezed past without even noticing us sneak up after him.

Once on the next floor, Sabina and I found ourselves in a storeroom. My eyes were so unaccustomed to the light that I winced as if in pain.

"Dead end?" Sabina asked.

I shook my head. "That wouldn't make sense. There's a way out of here, somewhere."

The storeroom was a giant pantry full of enormous cans of olives, great vats of maraschino cherries, and other super-sized containers of beverage garnishes. I noticed a curtain off to one side and peeked out. I waved Sabina over and, as she poked an eye through a gap in the cloth, I had to elbow her to stop her squealing. We were gazing into the VIP area, mere inches away from where Dave stood. Had we dared, we could have pinched a frontman buttock.

It was almost as if the storage closet had been built for spying. The curtain was made of double material, which meant we could wrap ourselves up and remain relatively hidden from both the VIP and waitstaff areas. Several times we heard waitstaff rummaging among the olives and cherries but no one ever caught onto our presence. We became so astute at hiding that servers would breeze past us, shoving our curtains aside, and were none the wiser that the material held two maniacal teenage girls.

"I can't believe that is him," Sabina said. "He is... right there. It can't be possible. This is what I've waited for all my life."

Despite having spent the past several days with Marta, the most fanatical of fans, I was surprised by the ardor of Sabina's words, at how intense her concentration was on this one object of desire.

Perhaps I wasn't seeing myself clearly, because everyone around me seemed hyper-focused on the less significant aspects of fandom. I'd been doing my best not to fall into their mindset, but I was finding it increasingly difficult to remain the sane, rational Devotee I'd been when I stepped off the plane.

But Sabina's words snapped me back. She and I were wrapped in grubby curtains that probably hadn't been washed in a decade, gazing in at a community we'd never fully be a part of, and she was declaring that moment the one she'd been waiting for all of her short years. As much as I wanted to step through that curtain and introduce Sabina to Dave, thus elevating her dreams to something akin to nirvana, I knew I couldn't risk it. I couldn't bear the humiliation of explaining to Bryan or Tommy that we hadn't been properly admitted and had to sneak through a pantry.

Dave was beyond sloshed. He slammed an empty champagne bottle onto the bar and was promptly rewarded with a full one, which he swilled as if his bodily organs depended on it. As he pressed the Dom to his lips, he took a small stumble backwards, his scrawny ass tottering directly towards me and my fellow pantry-lurker. As I whipped the curtain to obscure our faces, Sabina held up a hand against the material at just the right level. Seconds later, the curtain gave under the weight of a teetering booty, and Sabina gave a helpful push back in the proper direction. When my father had agreed to foot the bill to Europe, I don't think his dreams included his youngest daughter hiding in a nightclub pantry surreptitiously fondling the rear ends of rock stars.

When the rustling of the curtain had subsided, Sabina held her hand up and gazed as if it hadn't been attached to her own body for the past eighteen years. "*Su culo,*" she whispered, as if unable to believe she'd touched one of the most sacred of bodily parts. "I touched his…"

Her eyes flickered, and for a moment I thought she would faint right there among the maraschinos and pitted olives. Knowing there was no way I'd be able to stash an unconscious body, I lifted her to her feet and hauled ass out of the pantry, down the staircase past a bewildered waiter, and back into the relative security of the main dance floor. Sabina still seemed on the verge of becoming catatonic, her hand outstretched so that she stared at it unblinkingly. I found a couch for us in a corner and sat her down.

"You want a drink?" No response. "Sabina? Sabina, I'm talking to you."

"Hmm?" Glazed eyes peered up in my direction but stared straight through me.

"You stay here." I motioned as if she were a Pomeranian I was leaving tied outside a storefront. "I'm going to the bar. You'll be okay? Alright, stay. *Stay right here.*"

She nodded then returned her focus to her splayed hand. I imagined she had plans of having it bronzed for posterity.

"*Una bebida muy fuerte, con mucha fruta.*" I rattled off my order as easily as if it were my name. I was certain Marta would have said my accent was improving. And although the bartender, not yet accustomed to my repeated visits, gave me a quizzical stare, the drink he poured was much to my liking.

"There you are," Marta said, grabbing my hand with such force that I spilled several precious drops of fruity liquid. "It's Bryan and Alan. They're *down here.*" Had I been an outsider, the urgency with which we spoke to each other about such matters might have induced near-hysterical laughter. Instead, stuck right in the thick of it, my heart began to beat in my ears, overcoming the pounding bass of the DJ's rhythm.

Marta led me around the bend in the bar, then stopped an appropriate distance away from where the Brit and his American bodyguard stood conversing. A step this way, an angle that way, and we had positioned ourselves perfectly within their eye lines, with only a small cluster of giddy bar patrons conveniently between us. Within moments, the gaggle of female admirers had moved away, revealing us just as Marta had planned. We played it cool, nursing our drinks and hardly even glancing in their direction. As far as we were concerned, we'd just wandered into this bar, to that very spot, without any hint that our musical idols were reveling inside. That's how cool we were playing it.

Or not. When I dared flash a glance in their direction, I saw Bryan grinning as if panning my performance. A second later he waved us over, and Marta and I did our best to approach as if the most beautiful man on the planet weren't standing directly next to the bodyguard from Detroit. I maintained eye contact with my American comrade but caught peripheral glimpses of Alan. I treated him as if he were an eclipse, too dangerous to view directly.

Bryan threw a friendly arm about my shoulder. "I'd like you to meet two of my friends," he said to DM's finest. "This is Marta and this"—did I detect a pause for emphasis?—"is Jenna."

Marta bristled at my side, but I completely forgot about her when Alan opened his mouth. My drink nearly slipped from my hand when I heard his words. "Yes, we've met."

He remembered me.

There were roughly two gazillion women in Pacha who were dying to get so much as a wink from this man, and not only was I being formerly introduced by his own bodyguard, but He. Had. Remembered. Me. I was memorable. To Alan.

I mumbled something in response, nothing terribly brilliant, but neither was it humiliating, for once. "Get these two whatever they'd like," Alan told the bartender.

Marta squeezed my hand gently. "He remembered you, Jenn." The smile inside me was too big to come out all at once, and so I let it escape in pieces, just the tips of my mouth turning upward, then my eyes as wide as drum pads. Marta shared in my elation. "He *remembered you.*"

But as fate would have it, a tour member of more important stature than two drooling fanatics came to coax Alan away for some business. This was probably for the better, as I hadn't yet regained the power of speech.

We sought out our entourage and found Sofia a few yards away from a frenetically dancing Martin, who had one fist in the air and blond curls flopping to a deep tribal beat. The minions about him mimicked his moves, but he was oblivious to any presence but the music and his drink. Unbeknownst to Sofia, she had her own admirers milling a safe distance about her. Marta and I happened upon her just as one lanky roadie was about to make his move, but he sank back into the crowd when his prey moved towards us.

By this point, I had been exposed to enough Spanish to pick up every fifth word. "There you are! I've been looking all over for you." Sofia continued swaying, not missing a beat. I readied myself to relay the story of the Alan encounter but stopped as she swayed her hips and tossed a casual question. "Where's Sabina?"

My heart stuck in my throat. I'd left her in some corner nearly half an hour earlier, and in my current level of intoxication, I couldn't remember which corner that was. "Oh no." My two words were enough to stop Sofia's hip grinding and she remained oblivious when the faces of her admirers soured as her performance ended. "I forgot where I left her. She was… a little shocked."

I quickly recounted our sojourn upstairs, feeling the heat rise off Marta's skin with each word. By the time I'd gotten to the point where Sabina molested Dave's derriére, steam was rising off her brow. But she managed to stifle her anger long enough to seek out her friend, who by now had reclaimed consciousness and staked out a clear view of Martin and his fist-pumping posse. When we found her, Sabina was leaning her head into her fist in repose, a bubble of elation protecting her from the nightclub chaos.

We passed the next hour alternating between approaching band members and tag-teaming for drink runs, until finally in the early hours of morning, we showed our first signs of fatigue. I glanced about at my fellow diehards and saw the droop in Marta's eyes, the deliberate slowness in Sofia's swaying, and a stifled yawn from Sabina. I was the first to admit defeat, albeit half-heartedly.

"I'm going to take a breather." I received three very confused stares in response. "*Estoy cansada. Voy a sentarme para un poco.*" They nodded in response then returned to their ritualistic movements.

With bleary eyes I made my way to the couches in the corner, where I'd abandoned Sabina a few hours earlier. The seats were all but empty as I strolled across the dance floor, now half as full of revelers as when we'd first arrived, and I marveled at the stamina of the Spaniards. It had to be the siestas, I decided, and there was no sense attempting to import such a cultural anomaly to my hometown. After all, New York reveled in being the city that never sleeps, and I doubted any of its denizens would tolerate an addendum to that motto. Napping, both the word and the practice, meshed with Manhattan's edgy, hardboiled reputation as much as it did with unicorns and lollipops.

As I neared the couches, I noticed a lone figure sitting smack dab in the middle of one, and when I realized who it was, I screeched to a halt. There was no way I could nonchalantly pop a squat next to Alan, even though our acquaintance went as far back as a whole four hours. I'd be forced to make conversation and, in my current state of sobriety, I'd be even more tongue-tied than normal—worse, I might even humiliate myself by gushing over his godliness.

I began to change course when I caught him looking at me. He now knew me, might even remember my name, so there was no way I could run away like a love-sick groupie. And so I continued my pace and, as gracefully as I could have hoped for, allowed myself to sink into the soft comfort of the leather couch.

"Hi," I said as casually as my hormones would allow.

"Hello again." He returned the smile, and I felt my innards melt down through my belly and straight into my toes, leaving me a quivering exoskeleton of empty flesh.

As per the rules of civilized conversation, it was my turn to speak, but I had to consider every word before it passed my lips, lest I make a complete doofus of myself in front of my idol and crush of a lifetime. This meant that, with my synapses firing slightly slower than usual, my next sentence was long in coming. But when I got it, it was brilliant.

"Want to dance?"

Or not.

Alan laughed. But it was not the hedonistic cackle I might have expected. I reminded myself that he was not a head cheerleader seeking to sap the life force out of a member of the nerd herd. His laugh was amiable, intending no harm.

"I'm so drunk I don't think I could stand." His smile dazzled in the nightclub lights, which, unlike the thinning crowd below, continued to flash and spin unexhausted, willing us both to get up and groove. In the black light, his teeth shone a comical ultraviolet and, when I looked down, I saw that my pasty legs were a similar hue. I tucked them under me, mortified at my skin tone after being in Spain for half a week.

The rules of propriety dictated that I once again continue the conversation, but I was saved from further humiliation by Martin, who flopped onto the couch on Alan's other side. "Excuse me," Alan said politely, and the two bandmates dove headfirst into a conversation obscured by layers of pulsating beats.

Rather than eavesdrop, I peered out at the dance floor, hoping to catch a glimpse of my companions. But my vision was so blurred by fruity drinks and lack of sleep that I couldn't make out the waiter in front of me when Martin stopped him for another round. Alan even ordered another drink for me and, despite the awareness I was well past my limit, I accepted. There was no possible way I could turn down a drink bought (albeit at an open bar) for me by any member of the band, let alone by the one who made my hormones hit high notes.

I waited for my drink, the cushy couch beneath me slowly sapping the last of my energy. I propped up my head with one arm, hoping to remain vigilant until the waiter returned, but the world around me grew increasingly dim. The last thing I remembered was Martin rising to return to the dance floor as Alan handed me my drink. Then the angels lifted me to heaven.

* * *

I opened my eyes to see the same decadent nightclub, a little less blurry but still just as thumpingly loud and boisterous, despite the thinned-out crowd. As I raised my head off the couch, I felt my cheek peel away from the leather, which was much firmer under my head than it was the rest of my body. A moment later I shot bolt upright as reality hit me like a charging bull. What should have been the culmination of a wickedly erotic dream took on a nightmarish form: I'd taken a siesta on Alan Wilder's lap. And drooled.

In the pulsating lights of the club, I could make out the faint residue that outlined where my face had so recently lain. I looked up to find Alan fast asleep, his head tilted back on the couch and his arms splayed to either side, and felt a rush of relief. A moment later, I'd unstuck the rest of my flesh from the upholstery and, without making too much movement, left the sleeping idol to his rest, his profile even more angelic in the tranquility of slumber.

I found Marta, Sabina, and Sofia resting their barking dogs at the far end of the bar. Marta sat up straight as I approached.

"How was the VIP room?" she asked, a bitterness belying her innocent question.

"Don't know," I answered, my ability to speak slowly returning. "Haven't been up there. But we gotta go. *Now.*" I was back in full-on New York mode, as impatient and finger-snapping as ever. "Come on, up and at 'em."

Sofia made as if to stand but fell back into the couch. "Oh, *no puedo.*" She closed her eyes and would have fallen right to sleep had I not lent a hand in raising her to her fashionably shod feet.

"*Bueno.* Now Sabina." It was a little harder waking the tired imp, but soon she too was standing and upright. Marta refused my help and rose on her own with little coaxing.

"What's the rush? I've still got half a drink." She took a tiny sip, her eyes telling me she was intent on getting every last peseta's worth.

"Here, I'll help with that." I grabbed her glass and swigged the remainder, one or two icy squares tracing a painful route down my esophagus.

Marta's glare told me she thought I'd been off whooping it up without her. "What's the matter, Zhane? You break up another band?"

I ignored her question and slammed the empty glass on the counter. "*Finito. ¡Vamonos!*" I hooked arms with Sofia and Sabina and began to exit. Marta followed, her reluctance dragging like a truckload of concert equipment.

I was unprepared for what lay beyond Pacha's exclusive doors. Like one of my beloved literary vampires, I recoiled from the blinding whiteness of the early morning sun and raised a protective arm over my eyes. My companions did likewise, all of us groaning and hissing in the international language of diehard nightclubbers.

"*Dios mio*, it's past rush hour," Sofia said with a glance to her watch. We were but meters from the entrance to the subway, where, much like in Manhattan, the last of the Spanish suits were rising from the underground. Their jobs, however, most likely encouraged siestas, not morning-long comas.

As we were about to cross the street and wait for the next train to Sofia's neighborhood, the doors to Pacha swung open, persistent rhythms rolling into the street with the stragglers who stumbled out. Marta caught her breath in a tiny gasp as she noted who was among them.

From out of nowhere, a gaggle of girls younger than ourselves descended upon Dave, pens and papers at the ready to capture their idol's signature. But the lead singer was hardly in the mood. I didn't quite understand how someone of his meager frame had sucked down two full bottles of champagne—and who knew what else—but the effects were obvious, and he howled and swung at his idolaters as if they were zombies seeking a post-club snack of alcohol-soaked grey matter. The girls recoiled, their faces a mixture of horror and disappointment, as Dave's bodyguard finally came between them, although it was unclear whom he was protecting. When the teenyboppers had disappeared, one of them in tears, Dave seemed to calm, although his eyes never lost their squinted, red-rimmed glaze.

He leaned against the façade of Pacha and lit a cigarette, the thick smoke enveloping him in the heat of the Madrid morning. Every manner, every movement was calculated, as if he were constantly before the lens of Anton Corbijn's camera. Despite his scrawny frame and scraggly, post-grunge mane, I finally caught a glimpse of the bad boy that Dave acolytes found so appealing. Marta's gaze was rapturous.

She neither turned her head towards me nor blinked an eye as she shoved the ticket into my hand. "Get it for me, Zhane. You promised." Her lips remained half parted, as if about to accept a holy wafer.

"No way," I said, crushing the ticket back into her hand. "You saw what just happened." More crew spilled out of Pacha, and I couldn't tell if Alan was among the throng. Either way, I wanted nothing more than to head back to Sofia's and crash on her floor, *pronto.*

Marta's head rotated slowly in my direction, so slowly and deliberately that I thought she meant to spew pea soup on me. "You *promised,* Zhane."

"I did no such thing." My voice was firm but low enough that no one else could hear. "This is neither the time nor the place. We'll get it at the next concert."

"No!" Marta stomped her foot and all heads turned in our direction. Sofia and Sabina slipped off to one side, wisely distancing themselves. "You promised you'd get his autograph! You *promised!*" As she shrieked her words, the stench of a night's worth of drink rolled off her tongue, and I assumed I wasn't any less pungent.

"Let's not make a scene." But the roadies and Dave were already enjoying the free show. Our argument went on another few minutes, during which I tried to convince Marta that even though I hadn't actually made such a vow, I would do my best at the next concert, and that our friends were patiently waiting for us to go home and get some sleep.

Just when I thought I'd be sleeping in an alley with newspapers for blankets, Marta gave in, wrenching her elbow from my grasp to join her friends. When I glanced back, I noticed Bryan among the crowd, and I blushed to imagine what he thought of such an adolescent scene. I could only hope Alan hadn't noticed, and that he wouldn't be sending me a dry cleaning bill.

9

awoke to the realization that I had no clue where I was. My first impulse was to check to make sure I hadn't left a ring of drool on a famous pair of leather pants and, finding the fabric below me not of dead animal nor containing a human leg, I breathed relief. I soon gathered that I was in a hotel, but I had no recollection of checking in, let alone slipping out of the previous night's party gear and into a makeshift pajama set of t-shirt and flannel boxers. Then slowly it came back to me.

When we returned to Sofia's apartment, where she'd invited us to sleep on the couch, it was to find her mother severely distressed, not just that her daughter had gone missing all night, but that she'd been in an outfit that consisted of little more than black plastic bin liners—short ones, at that. Against such berating, the most fashionable of our foursome couldn't muster the strength to ask permission to have houseguests, so Marta and I hurriedly gathered our bags and scurried out the door, the sounds of generational warfare chasing us down the marble corridor.

Without even looking at a rate card, we checked into the closest hotel and promptly fell into a deep slumber, which is the state my traveling companion was still in when I rolled over and spied her snoring in the adjacent bed of the darkened room. I smacked my lips, shuddering at the stale residue of twelve straight hours of clubbing, and forced myself into the bathroom for a much-needed washing-up. By the time I came back into the bedroom, Marta was showing the first signs of stirring.

"*¿Que hora es?*" I had to assume she was still half-asleep as I doubted she would have asked me even this most basic of Spanish phrases.

"*A las siete,*" I responded, then for clarification added, "at night."

Her head swung toward me—too fast, I could tell, because a moment later she was cradling it in her hands. "*¿Noche? ¿Segura?*" I couldn't have imagined her voice any raspier, but it now sounded like someone running gravel over a grater.

"*Si, claro. Mira.*" I threw open the curtains so that the last rays of day burst into the room with blinding force. Marta threw her face on the pillow with a vampiric shriek of pain, and after a moment's hesitation, I drew the curtains shut.

While Marta convalesced, I took the opportunity to scribble in my journal all that had transpired over the last several days. With only the sound of our breath and my pen scratching away, it was the quietest moment Marta and I had yet spent together.

I finished up my entry while she took her turn cleaning up, then we were off to the lobby to pay our bill—not as outrageous as I'd feared—and to locate the nearest cafetería. Although my gums had only partially healed from my last bocadillo con queso, my queasy stomach was looking forward to something dry and crusty to soak up the remainder of the alcohol.

We sat at the counter chewing our food, too hungover and too stubborn to discuss the events of the previous night. Without the buffer of other people, the silence weighed upon us as heavily as the oppressive Spanish heat. I'd already learned that few buildings in the country were equipped with air conditioning, either because they were too old or the populace was too collectively obstinate to admit it was so damn hot. Even though it was early evening, it was still muggy enough for sweat to trace paths down my back and brow, which only added to my discomfort.

Marta washed down her final bite with a gulp of Orangina and rose to leave, but I remained seated, quietly finishing my bocadillo and picking at the few last crumbs to cause her further consternation. When at last I'd finished, I followed her silently out of the modest establishment and back into the bustling street, the city once again coming to life as the sun prepared its late departure. I didn't question where Marta led me. I knew that soon we'd be en route to Barcelona for the next concert. Whether that would be via train, bus, hot-air balloon, or covered wagon, I had no clue. But I'd be damned if I'd give Marta the satisfaction of asking.

As dusk descended and muted the city's vibrant colors, Marta piloted us down narrow alleys, across sweeping plazas, and past several metro stops that undoubtedly could have accelerated our progress. I was both surprised and pleased at the Zen-like patience I'd found deep within me, and I used our wanderings as an opportunity to take in the sights of a city I'd seen so little of. More than once I got caught up in sightseeing and almost lost track of my guide, the back of her dark-haired head blending in with the rest of the crowd so that I thought I'd strayed too far. But then I'd spot her just up a ways, and by the steadiness of her gait I knew that she was certain I was still behind her, even though I never saw her turn to check that I was following.

We soon arrived at our destination, and I marveled that no matter what city I visited, every bus terminal smelled equally as wretched. I caught up as Marta perused a schedule and, still ignoring me, approached the ticket counter. She rattled off her destination in Spanish, but I managed to decipher that she'd purchased only one ticket. Without casting a glance in my direction, she turned and took a seat on a nearby bench, leaving me to fend for myself. *No problemo.*

"*El mismo.* The same," I said to the clerk.

A moment later and I was seated on the same wooden bench a comfortable distance away from Marta, my face beaming that I'd beaten her with two simple words.

After writing postcards to kill the hour before our bus left, I boarded behind Marta. When she accidentally passed our row, I used the opportunity to snag the window seat, and she begrudgingly took the aisle. A rear-bound passenger conked her in the head with a duffel bag, and I had to turn my gaze out the window and stifle a chuckle.

The bus belched its goodbye to the Madrid depot, and Marta and I were once again on the road, the cover of night tempering the tension. I rolled up a shirt and propped it against the window for a pillow, preparing to take another siesta, when the passenger in front of me reclined his seat, whacking me in the kneecaps. I let out a yelp, the tenderness from a recent knee dislocation still quite fresh, but the man made no move to raise his seat. I attempted a few passive-aggressive maneuvers, including shoving the seatback, but to no avail.

My knees began to throb from the pressure, and despite every attempt to stop them, tears welled in my eyes, as much from frustration as from the pain. I had just given up and was about to attempt to get some sleep when I was surprised by Marta's voice. She was tapping the man in front of me, rousing him from slumber to get his attention. From what I could make out, she tried to speak reasonably with him, explaining my injury and that he was causing me great discomfort, but he wouldn't budge. She slumped back into her seat with a look of disgust.

"Thank you," I said.

She shrugged. "I didn't accomplish anything."

"Yeah, you did."

We exchanged bemused smirks and, just like that, all was forgiven.

"Switch seats with me." Marta stood in the aisle so I could get out.

"Then you'll have to deal with Señor Asshole." I didn't care if he understood English. Hell, I'd have been happy if he heard the insult.

"Get your overly long American legs out of there and let me and my stumpy ones sit behind Señor Asshole." She snapped her fingers and I knew she wouldn't sit until I'd obeyed. Once we'd swapped and were again reasonably comfortable, Marta rested a hand on my arm. "I'm sorry."

"Stop it."

"And I wanted the window anyway."

"You're an ass."

The bus engine muffled our laughter. Marta, however, wasn't done and she gave a quick shove to the seat reclining inches from her nose. Señor Asshole twitched and shot us the evil eye between the seats, but he didn't dare cause a scene. My laughter came out in a single loud snort through my nose, and Marta nearly lost her composure.

When a passenger returning from the bathroom smacked me in the head with her purse, the game was up. With no concern for those sleeping about us, we split the air with unrestrained cackles.

* * *

I had loved Madrid, what little I'd seen of it, but from the moment we set foot in Barcelona, I was enchanted. After failing to fall asleep on the bus—we'd slept most of the day, after all—Marta had spent the majority of the ride briefing me on the Catalonian city. "It is wonderful, yes. There's a reason Barcelona"—she of course pronounced it *Barthelona*—"was chosen to host the '92 Olympics. It is international, cosmopolitan, and, beyond all, beautiful." But she couldn't resist adding a zinger. "But of course, it is not Madrid."

During my bus-ride orientation, I learned more than a little Barcelona history, a smattering about its culture, and just enough of the dialect to irritate the natives. Spanish classes in American institutions tended to focus on the history of Latin American countries, with only a brief visit—usually around the time of the sailing of the Nina, Pinta, and Santa Maria—to the Iberian Peninsula. Marta imparted more information on Spain during our multi-hour bus ride than I'd ever learned in a classroom, although I was well aware that my lesson was far from objective.

First and foremost, Spain was continually getting shafted, its European peers holding it in much the same light that New Yorkers saw Staten Island: a barely tolerated slice of land that was fine to visit and exploit—especially exploit—but which would never be given the stature of its more powerful neighbors. Part of this disparagement was rooted in the country's own inability to get along. Castile, Catalonia, the Basque region—all were engaged in persistent in-fighting that pre-dated Franco's rise to power. Catalonia wanted independence, but, according to Marta, the capital was reluctant to liberate the now-prospering region because it had poured such immense financing into Catalonian industries and infrastructure since the time the region's economy was still in its infancy. As a vehemently independent teenager whose parents were paying enormous sums for out-of-state tuition, I could only concur with the Catalans.

"They want everything," Marta fumed. "We gave them everything and they still want more!" She patted her cheek with her hand to demonstrate what she thought of the Catalans. "They are Spaniards, yes, but they do not see it that way. To them, they are Catalans, and Catalans only. Spain be damned!"

Marta's diatribe no doubt disturbed Señor Asshole's sleep, but neither of us cared. In fact, we considered it a battle victory each time we caught his hairy eye flash between the seatbacks. "He's probably Catalan," she whispered, with the familiar cheek pat. "Always expecting more than he deserves." She gave the back of his seat a quick but forceful nudge before wresting her legs out from under it, then continued with her lesson. Marta had already recounted several stories of her beloved King Juan Carlos I, but for this occasion she drew upon her favorite.

For weeks before the '92 Olympics, held just the previous year, Spain had been abuzz with speculation over how the king would make his remarks at the opening ceremonies: Would he give them in the pure Spanish, Castilian, or would he speak in the region's native tongue? Marta's admiration of his diplomacy shone as she recounted his decision.

"We were all watching, all of the Iberian Peninsula—even Portugal, I'm sure. The whole country was glued to their televisions, as if our king's very words were more important than even the outcome of the World Cup. Imagine: The solidarity of an entire nation rested on whether he would say, 'Bienvenido' or 'Benvingut.'" The latter was spat, as if to rid her tongue of a foreign hair. "We waited, and we watched, and we waited." I emphasized with the poor Spaniards—Castilian and otherwise. "Then our king approached the podium, and he looked out on all of us, even those of us far away in our living rooms. And I knew by the look in his eyes that he would make the right decision. And he did."

I waited for her to continue, but she sank back against the window as if having reached the end of her story. "And?"

Marta shrugged. "And you know how it ends."

"Uh, no, I don't." I leaned forward, my body language imploring her to finish what she'd begun. "What the hell happened? What did he say?"

"Did you not watch the Olympics? Did you not hear our great king—?"

"What the hell did he say?"

Her expression seemed to convey the message that Europeans were right: We Americans were as uneducated and uninformed as they'd been led to believe. But she was Spanish. She had survived fascism—or at least its wake, having been born at the tail end of it—and so could certainly tolerate a little American impatience and ignorance.

"He is the wisest king ever. He welcomed the world in Catalan, and the whole of the stadium exploded when their language was recognized. It was unbelievable, Zhane. I felt the rumbling in Galicia." Emerald eyes defied me to doubt her. She then continued in a tone I'd thought existed only in made-for-TV movies, but Marta somehow managed to make it sound sincere. "I felt my heart sink a little when

I heard those first words. But a few moments later, he was speaking in Castilian, and I felt whole, truly Spanish, again."

I couldn't begin to comprehend Marta's adoration for her king, and it wasn't simply because I, an American, had been raised in a country that had hosed the idea of a monarchy as one of its founding tenets. I merely had no love for authority, let alone unelected authority figures who sponged off lesser folk to maintain their wealthy lifestyles.

It was evident by her stories that Marta's admiration stemmed not simply from his position of royalty and diplomatic skills but also from his overt playfulness. She happily—and proudly—recalled how the newspapers liked to follow the king on his beloved biking excursions, and how quite often he would race the paparazzi—more for the sport of it than because he wished to be left alone. More than once these pictures had appeared in the paper, the king beaming as he took a strong lead ahead of his pursuers. I suspected it was this duality—the tactful politician with a bent for mischief—that was the main attraction for Marta and her countrymen.

From politics, our talk soon turned to family, another topic I'd hoped to avoid, but one that was also quite dear to Marta's heart. Despite the disregard she'd shown her parents in lying and running away with her pen pal, she actually held them in high esteem and recounted gleefully the stories of her father's sense of humor or her mother's unwavering support of her children, no matter what other shortcomings she might have bestowed upon them.

The familial stories I'd so far recounted to Marta consisted mainly of my relatives' many eccentricities, namely those of my father. When it came to my mom, the tenuous relationship most adolescents shared with their parents was exacerbated by a failure to communicate and differences greater than those caused by a simple generation gap. We loved each other, despite the fact we hardly knew each other.

The incident with the ticket for smoking was one example. Had my mother found the ticket rather than my father, the ensuing argument would have been much more volatile, and I couldn't say for sure that I would have been allowed to leave on my vacation, no matter how much money had already been spent. It wasn't so much that my mother would have seen my transgression as unforgivable, but that I had violated the terms of our agreement that had allowed me to live in Manhattan, which my mother already saw as an act of defiance. Ironically, what I saw as the catalyst for my desire for independence stemmed from my mother: I became a latchkey kid in fourth grade when she took on a full-time job at the humane society where she'd been volunteering for more than a decade. I never begrudged her not being at home when I returned from school, or for having to care for the more than a dozen animals before I'd even started my homework. Rather, I was thankful that she had trusted me at such a young age, and I was certain that the resulting responsibility and solitude led to my craving even more independence.

My mother also could not—or would not, I often believed—reconcile with my vegetarianism, and on this point Marta sided with my mother, finding my unwillingness to sample some of Spain's great national dishes offensive, or at the very least impolite. I explained that most of my life I'd found it hypocritical that, after a day of helping my mother on her many "cat jobs," saving helpless creatures, I'd return home to eat a meal of dead animal. The love of animals had been instilled in me since I was old enough to bottle-feed a baby raccoon, and at 17, it had blossomed to the next step. I'd fought with my mother over my refusal to eat the meals she'd toiled to create. In her stubbornness, she continued to slide meat onto my plate long after

182

I'd informed her of my new, flesh-free diet, and would then become insulted when I'd make a whole new plate.

It was as if she resented the seeds she'd planted in me, and that she now saw my independence and newfound ethics as weeds that required eradication. To me, however, they were the blooms I most treasured, and the ones I planned to nurture the rest of my life.

My mother and I had hit a particularly rocky point in our relationship when I decided to spend my first summer home from college in Manhattan, only an hour from the family's Long Island homestead, but a world away to my mother, who had visited The City perhaps half a dozen times in the previous decade, three of which were to see *Cats*. She resented my father for granting me permission, even though his main reason for allowing me was because I'd never before spent a significant amount of time with Ilene, my half-sister who had grown up with her mother. For my father, it was a dream come true to have his two children finally live together under the same roof, even if that roof wasn't his. But my mother saw it only as my latest attempt to escape her authority and, although she tried not to show it, was hurt by my wish to both flee the nest as quickly as possible and establish a relationship with a family member to which she herself had no blood ties.

Marta and I chattered on into the night, exchanging broken-heart woes, snort-inducing escapades, and tales of fanatical music transgressions, the majority of which were centered around our most beloved of bands. I spilled to Marta about how, after years of being wrongly accused of doing so, I had finally fooled around with a friend's boyfriend. Marta didn't judge, simply nodded her head and listened unblinkingly. I'd had feelings for Sebastian for years, I told her, and Althea had told every one of our mutual friends that she knew we were going behind her back, despite having no evidence. I could only hope they knew me better than that.

"I was getting blamed," I explained. "She treated me like I was guilty even though nothing ever happened. But I wasn't having any of the fun." I added the latter with a wry grin, knowing full well that my dirty-minded friend would understand. "So, after years of being accused, we finally did something about it. Now, the only problem is, I'm sure she's found out. And when I get back, all my friends will know and I'll be ostracized." I thought of Dimitria, Althea's cousin and one of my closest friends, and imagined her hanging up when I tried to call and explain. "Almost makes me not want to go back home... ever."

"You should move to Spain," Marta suggested. "That would solve several problems. You can avoid your friends and, when you finally move back to Manhattan, it won't seem so far away to your mom." A fine suggestion, I conceded, but one made impractical by my lack of a Spanish passport. "You can marry Estevo," she said, offering up her younger brother, whom I'd yet to meet. Her eyes widened as the plan took hold. "Then we'd be family!" I couldn't tell whether or not she was kidding.

As the bus reached the city limits, Marta's face grew somber. "It's our last concert, Zhane, we have to make this one count."

The thought hadn't occurred to me. After this, the band took off for Germany, where they wouldn't play until the middle of the following week. Not only did I not want to spend the rest of my money traveling to another country, but I was due in France in only a few days and was looking forward to being united with Marion, whom I'd dubbed my "French sister" just the summer before.

"Let's write them a letter, Marta. Tell them what we've been through, what we've done just to see them, how much their music means to us." I began digging in my bag for paper and pen, purposely nudging the seats ahead of me so that Señor Asshole mumbled Spanish obscenities even as he slept. Marta had seemed on the verge of dozing off, but the idea now had her upright and alert. "How often do you get the chance to hand-deliver a fan letter to your idols?"

*　*　*

I'd heard many people extol Barcelona's beauty, but none of that beauty was to be found at the bus terminal. Marta and I untangled ourselves from the cramped bus seats and, our muscles still in need of a good stretch, all but stumbled down the stairs and into the glaring light. The sun had barely been up long enough to shed a glow let alone scorch us, and we took pleasure at being in the relative coolness while we could.

We found our way to an outdoor café, where Marta's Barcelonan friends sat awaiting our arrival. After the obligatory cheek-kissing, Sofia, Alberto, and Marta set off, the American following behind as the old friends caught up. As we wandered further into the city, I began to understand why Barcelona had received such praise from everyone who visited. The architecture was just as I'd envisioned all of Europe to be. Winding alleyways were enclosed by tall, terraced buildings so close to one another that it gave the impression of a canyon, while small balconies with brightly colored shutters overflowed with greenery. Even the most common residences had an aura of stateliness, in part due to the ornate facades that would be far too expensive to commission in the modern era. Although I couldn't tell the age of the buildings, I guessed that most were at least a couple hundred years old, especially those we passed on the main boulevards. Contemporary architecture was rare, with only a few newer constructions standing out amid their better-dressed neighbors.

I was soon informed that we were headed to the heart of the city, Las Ramblas, a street so incredibly stunning that my guides would be remiss as Barcelonans if I left without seeing it. I was far from disappointed.

We turned onto a shaded boulevard divided straight down the middle by a tree-lined pedestrian walkway, so that even though the street was wide, cars were forced into a single lane on either side. Color-spewing stalls sold any trinket you could need or want—maps, flowers, fruits, umbrellas, books, even parakeets. For once I was glad that the Spanish walked at such a slow pace. While my group strolled along, I could duck into a stall just long enough to browse and still catch up.

But when Marta and friends decided it was time again to stop for coffee, less than two hours after our last, I opted to head out solo and hit the shops. I'd been in the same clothes the last several days and, although I'd rinsed them several times, I was feeling rather ripe and in need of a fresh outfit. Marta seemed puzzled that I didn't want to sit and listen to them chat about people I'd never heard of and would never meet, but she merely gave a shrug and told me she'd meet me in an hour and a half.

That gave me more than enough time to find the perfect ensemble for my last night backstage. Although I could tell Las Ramblas and the surrounding area were on the pricier side, I also knew that this meant I'd have a wider variety of stores close at hand. A warmth against my thigh where my money lay in my pocket said it was time to shop, and not a second later I was inside the closest boutique.

I had a vague idea what I was looking for. Something fun but that still showed class. Definitely a skirt, but nothing slutty or too short that would classify me as a tour whore. An outfit I could wear in Manhattan without looking like I'd just stepped off the boat. And, above all, something that wouldn't cost more than $200 American, including shoes. The final part was the kicker, since every price tag I'd turned over left my eyes bulging at the multiple digits, even after I'd done the conversion.

The shopkeepers, who could apparently detect my forehead sign, which still glowed neon-bright even after a week in Spain, followed me around the shop offering assistance, but few spoke enough English to understand the fine nuances I required in an ensemble. After searching through nearly half a dozen shops, I gave up hope of finding someone who understood me and concentrated on making myself understood. If I could successfully order a flesh-free meal or convey the need for a fruity cocktail in Spanish, surely I could communicate my couture requirements. I racked my brain for vocabulary I hadn't used since my eleventh-grade finals, stuttering like an imbecile to any salesgirl with enough patience to tolerate a fixated American.

My face aglow with both pride and joy, I returned to the café at the appointed time to show off my new threads. Marta fingered the material of my cream-colored belted vest, checked the tag of the black pleated shirt, and deemed both satisfactory. In the next breath, she announced that it was time for lunch. Much like hobbits, the Spanish seemed to divide the day into back-to-back meals, with hardly a pocket of time not devoted to ingesting either food (daylight hours) or libations (evening). Moments later, I found myself in a Burger King and realized I'd eaten at more American fast-food chains in the past week than I had in the last year (Taco Bell notwithstanding, as it was practically connected to my dorm and was, therefore, a de facto cafeteria).

Between bites of fries and nips of Coke—the only two items on the menu not laden with animal byproducts—I scribbled several letters to friends. Then, just when I thought we'd be having our dinner at the same table where we were lunching, our party rose with an announcement from Marta that made my heart sing. "*Vamanos,* we're going shopping."

I'd been worried that she hadn't heard me lament my lack of proper footwear for the evening, but Marta was full of surprises as she led me to El Corte Inglés, a multi-level department store that she promised would have the shoes of my dreams. Within fifteen minutes I'd located the cutest, strappiest pair of non-leather black shoes, the two-inch heels double-dog daring me to wear them on the cobblestone streets. Marta, not knowing that my obsession for footwear was only slightly less fervent than that for Depeche Mode, commented that the devilishly cheerful grin I wore was new to her, and that I should most certainly make it part of my outfit when I bid farewell to Alan. My knees buckled at the mention of his name, and I recalled our last encounter and the resulting drool marks, shuddering in embarrassment even though I hadn't told a soul about my impromptu napping place.

We continued our promenade down the length of Las Ramblas, Sofia and Alberto pointing out key landmarks—a façade by Gaudí, a mosaic by Miró. The city was a wealth of architectural and artistic wonders, even under our feet. But Marta and I trumped our guides when we spotted Fletch strolling the boulevard. As we passed him, he gave a salubrious "Hello" and nodded in our direction. Marta and I returned the greeting, then continued calmly on our way.

Sofia and Alberto all but fell at our feet. We'd not only been recognized by their chosen royalty, we'd been *acknowledged.* Little did they know how much willpower had been put into maintaining our nonchalance.

Marta checked her watch and found that we had only a few hours before curtain, and, as usual, we'd have to arrive early. We hightailed it to the nearest bus station, where we swapped sweaty clothes for fresh evening gear, then trotted to the lockers to stash our bags. *"¡Joder!"* Marta's second-favorite phrase, after *puta madre*, was repeated several times as she searched unsuccessfully for a working locker. "They are all broken. And we cannot bring our bags into the stadium. We have no choice."

And so, to the other side of town we raced, hoping that the lockers at the other bus station would be in working condition. No sooner had our pesetas clinked to the bottom of the metal storage units then we were off, my two-inch heels hardly hindering me in my race for the nearest metro.

Although it brought us clear across the city, the subway dumped us a good distance from the stadium, and as I sized up the mini-mountain before me, I made an executive decision—or, rather, my feet did. "I'll spring for a taxi."

Marta shrugged. "It's only a twenty-minute walk. You don't need to—"

But I was already hailing a cab. With deliberate slowness, as if taking a taxi were a gauche form of transportation suitable only for tourists, Marta climbed in beside me and gave the driver instructions. It was then that I first witnessed the infamous Catalonian rivalry, as the driver gave us an unmistakably surly gaze in the rearview mirror, then proceeded to take his time driving up the hill.

"You see?" Marta whispered under her breath. "He heard my accent. He knows I am Spanish but not Catalan."

Although we weren't nearly as pressed for time as we would have been had we walked, I decided to speed up the process. *"Por favor, hay un concierto a las ocho."* I continued to ramble a lengthy excuse, not bothering to conjugate properly and peppering my speech with enough "uhs" and "ums" to convey I was not only a foreigner but possibly a mentally challenged one at that. The result was just as I'd hoped. The driver, not wanting to offend *la americana*, raced us up the hill to the gates of the Anella Olímpica, the ring enclosing the sports facilities used for the '92 Olympics.

We sailed past palatial buildings and shady gardens brimming with color. The city of Barcelona spread out below us as we rose higher up Montjuïc, affording a panoramic view that I would not have appreciated as much had I been hoofing it in heels.

"Whatever this ride costs, it'll be worth it," I told Marta as the sun glinted off various rooftops, spires, and communication towers. Six hundred feet higher and only twice as many pesetas later, we arrived.

The line seemed eternal, and despite the beauty of the Olympic Village, I felt my heart sink when I saw the throngs already waiting. Etiquette be damned, I was a New Yorker, and I wasn't going to spend my last concert in nosebleed seats. I held Marta's hand and, muttering courteous but incorrect Spanish phrases of politeness, I wove a path through the sweaty bodies and managed to place us but four rows from the front of the line. When a dark-haired fan grumbled words I took to be aimed at us, I turned and, with my sweetest smile, asked him in halfway decent Spanish to repeat, as the poor American couldn't hear very well.

The Catalonian held up a hand in apology and gave me a quizzical smile, as if trying to peg the accent. Marta spun me back around by grabbing my elbow.

"We're here for one reason, remember." As if I could forget.

As the hour wore on, the overheated crowd grew more restless, and we were often carried from side to side in a wave of human bodies that undulated based on whim. Refrains of the Complaining Song wafted towards the front of the crowd every so often, during which time the masses swayed in rhythm to their favorite of tunes. Marta and I interlocked our arms to prevent being split up in the crowd, but that soon became uncomfortable as we were pressed forward into the bodies ahead of us. I used the added height from my heels to peek over the crowd and report updates to my slightly shorter friend. At one point, the mass of humans surged forward so fiercely that she was certain we were being let in, but I informed her it was just the security guards changing posts.

I watched the gates to the Olympic Ring open and close several times, and with each passing of security, the crowd assumed this was the moment and strained forward against the multitudes blocking their path. There at the front of the line, Marta and I felt the shoving of thousands as we were unwillingly thrust into the strangers ahead of us. Had I fainted from the heat, the masses about me would have kept me upright.

"You know the drill," Marta said, gripping my arm in hers. "When the gates open, run to the stadium. It's not far."

"Not far?" I peered over the heads in front of me, expecting to see a building just beyond the heavily guarded iron gates but saw only trees. I felt a single bead of sweat roll down my back and get absorbed by the liner of my new sleeveless vest. "It's not right there? Just inside?"

Marta shrugged. "I don't know how far exactly, but it's… not far. A hundred meters at most." Even that was too far with this crowd, especially in heels.

Golden hues fell across the landscape, gilding the scenery. I found it hard to imagine that the Olympic Village, although obviously used for other special occasions such as this one, had been built primarily for a one-time event, even for something of such international importance. With my arms folded against my chest, I took another peek at the gates and noticed security pushing the hordes back behind crowd-control barriers, the same kind Marta and I had squatted on days earlier at the Pontevedra concert. My ass winced in memory of the waffle marks it had bore from having sat on those grates for hours. Once the gate opened, we'd have to first pass around the barriers, then rush through the gates and across the open plaza, where we'd finally have our tickets checked. Once inside the Palau Sant Jordi, there'd be one last sprint across the stadium floor, and my work would be done. I prayed that the plaza courtyard was flat cement and not uneven cobbles, or I'd find myself with a turned heel.

The noise of the crowd grew from a steady drone to an incessant roar and once again I felt the throngs swell forward, this time with cause: The gates were opening. I readied myself for the sprint, but before I could move, the crowd heaved forward so quickly that I didn't have room to move. I heard screams ahead of me and a great clattering of metal as I pitched forward, my arms unable to grab anything for balance. The world went horizontal as I fell, my face mashed against the back of a stranger until, with a horrible thud, we hit the ground simultaneously. His body had softened my fall, but I still felt a surge of pain, and I could only imagine what it must have been like to hit the concrete with the weight of another person on top of you. A second later, I had a better idea as a falling body knocked the air out of my lungs and remained collapsed across my back.

The thud of another impact followed and I lost the ability to see as limbs and clothing covered my eyes. My arms were trapped beneath me, so I couldn't even move forward or attempt to push myself out from under the human dogpile. When a high-pitched scream pierced through the layers of people on top of me, I tried to get a hold of the thoughts in my head, tried to determine the best course of action, despite being able to do little more than lie as still as if I'd been embedded in cement.

The bodies rolled off and I could see again, but as I tried to raise myself with my arms, the next wave of racing fans tore past and knocked me down again, this time onto the crowd-control barriers, which were now lying useless on their sides. My head slammed into the metal and for a moment my vision blurred, but I still managed to find the strength to push off the ground with my hands, only to get kicked aside in a twisted mass, an army of fans marching over my limbs. A few people in the stampede tried to reach down to help me up, but they were soon swept away by the river of bodies.

I tried screaming in English for help, then had the sense to change my appeal to "*¡ayúdame!*" Each time I tried to stand up or crawl away to escape the advancing feet, I was stomped back to the pavement, my head and legs crushed against the bars of the barrier again and again. I glanced around for Marta, but she was nowhere to be seen.

After what seemed like an eternity of struggling, I gave up. I could no longer fight, and it seemed the pain was worsened every time I tried to free myself from the pile of bodies on the ground. One more foot stomped on the side of my face, another trampled my arm, and I let it lay where it had been kicked. I felt the warmth of blood pouring down my leg, I was certain I had broken at least one finger, and my eyesight was hazier than after a pub crawl with Tommy. Just as I'd resigned myself to being crushed, I felt two strong hands tuck themselves under my arms and drag my body out of harm's way.

Once at a safe distance, the line still swarming ever past me, I wobbled to my feet, exhausted but conscious. Still out of breath, Marta asked if I was okay.

With deliberately slow movements, I gave my body a once-over. I was dirty, wrinkled, and bleeding. The nail on my big toe had broken off almost to the quick. My legs, still throbbing in the places where they'd been crushed against the bars of the metal barrier, were badly scraped and had rivulets of blood tracing paths through the dirt. My head beat a steady rhythm in time to the pulsing in my legs. As I watched the last of the fans trickle peacefully by, I stood not quite believing what had happened or that I was still alive.

"Yeah, I think I'm okay." My voice sounded like someone else's. It took me a moment to realize it had actually been me replying.

Marta and I exchanged uneasy smiles. "Thought I'd lost you there for a minute. You didn't move for a long time." She rubbed my arm, a tender gesture that caught me off guard.

"Kind of hard with so many bodies on top of you."

"Does make the task a little more difficult." She let out a long breath, shook out her arms, and gave a self-satisfied clap, like a counselor encouraging her campers to weave those lanyard keychains faster. "Now, let's get our tickets."

Too stunned to argue with such doggedness, I limped behind her to will-call, where our day only worsened. Within moments, Marta was quarrelling with the clerk at the top of her lungs, unaware of the gawkers passing by.

"They claim they don't have our tickets," Marta told me, as if a deaf mute couldn't have deciphered her hysterical gesturing and reddened face. "You try."

And so we attempted our latest scheme: the American acting as ambassador between the Catalonian and Galician. But we were not graced with the same luck as with the cabbie.

"They don't have them, Marta. He's not playing with you." Marta seethed, but the energy to calm her had been stamped out of me. We began the slow, painful walk to the entrance to the Palau Sant Jordi, our ordinary *admisión* tickets in hand.

The floor of the stadium was already brimming with Mode-hungry fans, offering no hope for the close-up encounter we'd enjoyed at the past two concerts. We spotted Sofia and Alberto in the stands about halfway back from the stage and joined them, reluctantly admitting defeat.

The show wouldn't start for at least another hour, and Marta and I sat in silence, dejection etched on our faces as the hordes buzzed with the same excitement we had felt in Pontevedra so long ago. But our own enthusiasm had dissipated, the stampede having sapped all the passion we'd built over the last week.

Pain throbbed in every joint of my body as if the rungs of the crowd-control barrier were still slamming against my legs. When I told Marta I was going to look for the first aid station, she wished me luck before I hobbled down the stairs in search of medical relief.

Not far from where I assumed the backstage party would be held later on, I found a long line of triaged fans with injuries ranging from scrapes that required a mere band-aid to oozing wounds that made me want to barf up my most recent bocadillo. The injured were so numerous that I thought for sure I'd miss Marxman's set, but when I swooned and reached out for a wall for balance, I suddenly found myself surrounded by swarthy nurse aids so dreamy they could have been cast as love interests in a Merchant Ivory film. I allowed myself to be laid on a bed while a particularly fine-looking specimen of a Barcelonan took my pulse. I held my breath, hoping the change in my systolic pressure would keep him at my bedside a little bit longer.

The Castilian accent only compounded my lack of Spanish comprehension, and when Señor Dreamboat asked where the pain was, I pointed to a place that would probably have required pixilation on American network television. The spot was on my outer thigh, which required lifting my trampled, four-hour-old skirt for observation, and with the limited privacy afforded by the makeshift triage shelter, all eyes were on parts of my body that many of my long-time doctors had never seen. I turned my head to the side and began counting stains on the ceiling to try to block the humiliation.

A flash of light brought me back to the present and I looked up to see a bloke with a camera shooting the scene, a videographer by his side. A murmur arose throughout the backstage ward and, after I'd deciphered the accent, I realized that I was being filmed, skirt up around my neck, by none other than Anton Corbijn. My posterior was being recorded for posterity, just to make up for the lack of record of my previous evenings of humiliation.

I tucked my skirt down, told Señor Dreamboat I was feeling much better all of a sudden, and hobbled out before my embarrassment reached proportions requiring years of professional therapy. Despite the pain and some nagging feeling that I couldn't pinpoint, I decided what I needed was a walk, and possibly some retail therapy. I wandered down the stands to the far end of the floor and was perusing the merch booth when I heard a welcome, familiar sound: American voices.

Putting my aches behind me, I struck up a conversation with two backpackers, whom I learned had purchased tickets for the concert on a whim that very day. They were effusive in their tale of how it had all come to be.

While wandering the streets of Barcelona, the Moder of the duo had spotted Fletch strolling Las Ramblas and, being a ballsy American, approached him. When I learned that they'd been rewarded for their boldness with backstage passes, I was relieved that Marta had remained in the stands. There was no telling how she might have reacted if she'd heard that two happy-go-lucky travelers, who hadn't suffered our many tragedies, had pulled off such a coup. I was equally thankful for her absence when I learned that one of the Americans attended Michigan State. After my diatribe about the Wolverine State's lack of importance, I'd run into more Michiganders in Europe than I ever had on the Ann Arbor campus.

Perhaps it was the near-death encounter, or the ease of communicating with people from my own country, or any manner of reasons, but at that particular moment, I needed to spill my guts. And spill I did.

I told these total strangers how empty I felt, how despite the elation of having survived a human stampede, I felt that something was still inexplicably *wrong*. I couldn't pinpoint exactly what, but I could feel it, like a nagging itch. I babbled for several minutes about the uneasy feeling in the pit of my stomach, a premonition of something bad still to come. My mouth raced so frantically that I was unmindful of their expressions, but had I noted, I might have stopped my insensible rant and assured them I wasn't on day leave from the asylum.

The Americans, arms loaded with Depeche swag, cast a final uncomfortable glance in my direction before excusing themselves. My despair had led me to alienating the only people I could commiserate with in my own language.

And so I climbed the staircase back towards Marta and her friends but continued onwards into the highest seats to a vantage point where I could gaze down on the milling crowds. As I sat in the dreaded nosebleed section, a loneliness like none I'd ever before experienced washed over me. In my darkest days of pseudo-gothdom, I had never felt such isolation. I wanted nothing more than to speak to someone, anyone I'd known for more than a week, someone familiar, someone who might possibly understand the various emotions that were wreaking havoc on my system. But I was alone, utterly alone—despite being surrounded by multitudes of like-minded individuals.

I rejoined the others only seconds before the concert began and Marta, sensing my conflicted emotions, took my hand in hers. Even after Marxman had left the stage, I still couldn't shake my funk.

Marta informed me that this concert was to be filmed by Anton Corbijn, and I refrained from telling her what else the photographer might have captured with his lens only a few moments earlier. His presence alone made the concert revelatory, but I couldn't dislodge my apprehension, even when it came time to make fun of Dave as he hammed it up for the cameras. At the previous concerts, I couldn't have imagined a more egotistical display, but Dave proved me wrong, strutting about as if the answers to the world's problems lay in the right amount of shaking his can.

By the fourth song, my spirits had lifted enough that I sang along, my voice carrying throughout the Palau Sant Jordi with the rest of the masses. And by the time the concert ended, I felt reformed, not quite my old self, but leagues ahead of where I'd been when the curtain first rose. Their music had always held this sway over me, lifting me out of the darkest pits of teen angst. Music was my addiction, which was, as far as I was concerned, a far better alternative than others I could have turned to.

Once outside the stadium, Marta fell into her predictable behavior. Despite every excuse I could conjure, she kept coming back with reasons why I should approach someone in security and beg for backstage passes. It wasn't simply my self-respect that prevented me from bothering the hourly wageworkers, although that was a good portion of it. I'd expected Marta to acknowledge my previous attempt at obtaining our coveted passes, but either she chose not to remember my encounter with the Swagman or she didn't consider it reason enough to abandon our quest. We were about to ditch all efforts of going backstage—and thus, once again proclaiming my foosball ineptitude—when I ran into Christiane.

My amiable French friend sought me out in the crowd and pulled me to the backstage entrance. "She's with me," she told the security guard, someone I didn't recognize and so presumed to be part of the local entourage. But he was having none of it and, seeing I lacked the provisional sticky placard on my clothing, would not allow me any further.

Christiane began a few words of apology, but I stopped her. "It's okay, you tried. Now go have some fun!"

She flashed a coquettish smile, then pulled me aside to whisper some last words of advice into my ear. "They'll return to their hotel for a drink before going to the next club. If you go there, you can ask Fletch where the after-party will be."

No sooner had the words left her lips than she was absorbed into the throngs of backstage partiers, her final counsel flitting through the air like the words of an oracle.

Marta and I fled in search of a taxi to take us to the Hotel Meridien. Even as we slid into the backseat of the cab, we knew we were in for the same inhospitable treatment Marta had warned me of. But in our rush, we forgot our plan to use me as good-will ambassador, and Marta jumped into her habitual role of tour guide. Her Galician accent was good enough reason for the cabbie to take us on a wild goose chase, the meter still running at more than double fare due to the late hour. When we realized what was happening, I hunched down in the seat and pulled Marta down with me. "Play along," I whispered. "Just do as I say." I knew it would be hard for her, but I also knew that the stakes were too high for her to disobey.

I held my stomach and began to groan, muttering under my breath what Marta should tell the cabbie. "I'm not feeling well," I coached her. "I'll be sick if I don't get to my hotel room soon."

Wary eyes flashed in the rearview mirror, and I continued my backseat performance. "Tell him I'll vomit all over his cab. I'm not going to make it."

My acting was effective, as I discerned from the heightened speed. But soon I found myself wondering if I was too good an actress when Marta bent to translate his latest concern.

"He thinks we should take you to the hospital," she informed me. "He says you don't look—how do you say?—long for this world."

I played up the resulting groan, drowning out my instructions to Marta that I, a pampered American, needed only my air-conditioned room at the Hotel Meridien and I would be recuperating in no time. He stepped on the gas, permanently embedding my head-print in the taxi seat back, even as the cabbie declared the Hotel Meridien nonexistent.

Moments after this utterance, we pulled up in front of our destination. Marta helped me out of the cab so gingerly that for a moment I thought she might have told him I was expecting. As she flung a handful of pesetas onto the passenger seat and I began a revelatory dance, the cabbie shot us a disdainful glance, flashed an unfriendly hand gesture, and sped off into the night.

We weren't the first to arrive. The front panes of the hotel bar were plastered with the adolescent noses of Spanish groupies intent on observing the band members in a zoo-like atmosphere, their idols engaged in naturalistic behavior just inches away behind the glass. I could only imagine what the scene was like from the other side.

Marta and I removed ourselves from the commotion by walking down to the corner and waiting out the chaos. At one point, the disorder became so great that Bryan had to come out and shoo away the riff-raff so that the band could have a few moments of privacy. I thought he spied us at the end of the block, and I was thankful that I wasn't among the throngs he was trying to keep at bay.

Moments later, two towncars with darkened windows sped by us, and Marta assumed they were those of Fletch and Martin. "They're off to the clubs!" Our corner location allowed us to grab a cab ahead of all the flailing wannabes. We had just slid into the backseat when Alan's car passed us.

"Follow that car!" we ordered in unison. We were equally surprised when the cabbie heeded our words. A heavy step on the gas let us both feel the pull of several Gs as our hired vehicle peeled away from the curb.

Not only was our cabbie well versed in cinematic cliché, he was also skilled in keeping a safe distance from the pursued car—even without Marta or I having to tell him so or feigning nausea. A few miles later, we found ourselves outside the landmark nightclub Studio 54, itself an homage to the infamous Manhattan club of the same name.

We rolled up right next to Alan's car, and I slunk down in my seat so that the most worthy of band members wouldn't see me. I elbowed Marta, telling her to have the cabbie go around the block to give us some breathing room while the band went inside. When I peeked through the taxi window, my stomach dropped at the sight of Bryan's back only inches away. I would've rather been caught in another stampede than have Bryan or any other bodyguard catch us tailing the band.

After security escorted our favorite foursome inside, Marta and I graciously tipped our cooperative cabbie before making our way past the bouncers. Studio 54 was on par with the most grandiose nightclubs of Madrid, with multiple levels of bars and dance floors teeming with Spanish fashionistas, as well as drink prices to match the hype. When we'd made several circuits of the club with no sign of the band, Marta glowered with the realization they must be ensconced in a deeper room than those we'd yet discovered. As upset as I was, and still aching from head to toe, I resolved to make the most of our last night on the lam. Tomorrow we'd be returning as civilians to León, and there was no telling what trouble awaited once we were finally under her parents' roof.

I spotted Christiane, whose address I'd been meaning to ask for. Not only did I enjoy the idea of having a French pen pal to share Depeche Mode stories with, but there was also the chance she lived near Marion and that, once I was in France, we could scour Parisian record stores for rarities and products that would have been import-only back in the States. After we'd exchanged contact information, I asked if she would mind delivering the letter Marta and I had written to the band. She disappeared upstairs, and Marta and I returned to the bar, fantasizing about how each of the members might react to our note. Entrenched in our daydreaming, I was surprised to feel a tap on my shoulder, and even more so when I saw that Christiane had returned.

"Come with me," she beckoned. "You can deliver the note yourself."

We both jumped forward, but Christiane's next words shot Marta down. "I'm sorry, I can only take one of you." The look on Marta's face pained me almost more than my missing toenail, but there was nothing I could do.

Once Christiane had led me past VIP security, she excused herself and slid into a booth next to Martin as if he were a high school chum. The two chatted amiably, and I felt a surge of jealousy at Christiane's fearlessness. I couldn't imagine behaving so nonchalantly with my idols, flopping down at their side, and talking as if they weren't the sole reason I had made it through high school without a running prescription for Prozac.

Through the black-garbed throngs, I spotted Bryan and thanked him again for letting us backstage that first night. "No problem," he said, surprising me with a bear hug. "I'll make sure you have passes in Frankfurt."

I felt my insides flip and considered the possibility of Marta and I prolonging our fugitive lifestyle for another week. Then that familiar knot of apprehension twisted in my gut.

"We won't be in Frankfurt." The words came out reluctantly. "This is our last concert. I just wanted to come up here to thank you. It really meant a lot to us." I did my best not to sound choked up and overly sentimental, no matter what my true emotions were. I hadn't yet reconciled that our adventure was ending. I knew we could have continued on, but that nagging itch told me that this would be the last stop of the tour.

"Maybe in Michigan then."

I forced a smile. "Yeah, maybe."

I was wandering around the room, looking for other acquaintances to bid farewell to, when I spotted Martin sitting on the floor, nary a groupie in sight. He was singing—not the tune blasting from the club speakers, but one playing in his head—and pumping his fist in time to the tempo of his internal DJ. I knew he never stayed in one place for more than five minutes, so I had to seize the opportunity.

I squatted down and handed him the note we had written. "My friend and I wrote this for you and the rest of the group." Using Christiane's boldness as an example, I tried to behave as if he were just an ordinary schmo, that I'd already had a thousand conversations with him, but I could still hear the stutter in my voice. "We just wanted to thank you for what was probably one of the best weeks of our lives."

Martin smiled, his eyes focusing not on me but on some faraway object the alcohol had attracted them to. "Okay, thank you." His head never missed a beat as he tucked the note into a black fanny pack, an accessory I found odd for a rock star of his stature. "I'll put it in me pouch and read it tomorrow." He gave me a last quick smile and polite nod, then returned to conducting the music in his head.

I roamed the room some more and found Christiane sitting in a recessed booth, a faraway look in her eyes. I sat next to her, not bothering to see who the dark figure seated in the shadows behind us was. She gave me a quick flash of recognition, then we both stared ahead and watched the giddy partygoers.

When next I turned towards Christiane, her head was in her hands. I couldn't tell if she was crying or resting, but I put an arm around her. Although I hardly knew Christiane, she had shown me kindness and helped me even though I'd been a perfect stranger—a fellow Devotee, yes, but a stranger nonetheless—and so I felt it only proper that I support her now. I asked if she would like to use the bathroom and, as I led her away, I turned to see who had been lurking in the darkness. It was Alan. My heart skipped a beat when I realized he'd been eyeing us the entire time. I managed an ungraceful smile as I led my tearful friend away.

Once in the harsh light of the bathroom, I began wiping away Christiane's smeared mascara with a wet paper towel, but she didn't wish to speak about what had upset her. I'd seen her earlier with two other young women, one of who resembled her enough that I assumed it was her sister, but I had no idea where they were now, and I couldn't get any information out of my mute friend.

When she was once again presentable, we rejoined the partiers on the second-floor balcony and stood watching the gyrating crowds below. I watched the spectacle of Studio 54 a few more moments before deciding to return to Marta. No doubt she'd be pouting in a corner, and I couldn't blame her.

I found my Spanish cohort on the bottom of the first-floor steps. Anger emanated like cartoon clouds. Neither of us spoke.

She moved to the rail and looked out onto the dance floor, one story below where Christiane probably still stood in the same posture. Despite the cartoon clouds, I knew there were other, similar emotions simmering within each of us. Even as we stood motionless, I could feel hers lapping over mine as if brought in by the tide, each successive set drawing us back to each other, reminding us that we had come for a common cause that we had fulfilled together, no matter what obstacles has been thrown in our path.

The lights pulsated around us just as they would have had I never left New York. I could have been in any nightclub anywhere in the world, but I had landed here because of a very particular mission, a mission greater than merely gaining VIP access. And we'd succeeded. Beyond our wildest dreams. Before leaving the States, the most I'd hoped for was a brief encounter with our muses, a chance to say hello to the artists who had given meaning to our teenage existence. The previous week had given us credence with idols (if only when it came to foosball proficiency) and a sense of belonging to a culture that meant so much more than some Greek letters on a sweatshirt. It was the first time that I truly felt as if I belonged to something that actually mattered, something that existed beyond the boundaries of my limited experience and that would continue to exist when I didn't show up backstage at the next concert. Like some fairytale world, the party would transport itself elsewhere and the reveling would continue, long after I had gone. It was far bigger than me, but I had been part of it, if only for a brief instant.

It seemed like we watched the crowds for hours, not a word passing between us.

Then I felt a tap on my shoulder. I turned and Marta was pointing to the third-floor balcony, where Tommy stood waving and motioning for us to come up. We met him at the stairs and, with our VIP host to guide us, breezed past the security guard as if we were as important as the rock stars within.

Once inside the safe harbor of the private party, Tommy told us we could get free drinks from the open bar. The serving wench, however, sensing that I wasn't a true part of the A-list, either didn't understand me or chose not to. After five minutes of trying to flag her down to order my usual fruity beverage, I glanced over at Tommy and shrugged. He encouraged me by shooing me with a flick of his hand to keep at it. Another five minutes later and I was ready to jump behind the bar and make the damn drink myself. I returned to Tommy's side, ready to complain about the horrid service, and realized at the last second that he was engaged in conversation with Alan.

My entire body tingled as if from lack of circulation, my head going woozy at the thought that Alan might hand me a dry-cleaning bill—or worse, the receipt for a new pair of leather pants because the drool stain wouldn't come out. I tried to play it cool.

"She won't even acknowledge me. I've been waiting and waiting and can't get a goddamn drink!"

Tommy shrugged, but Alan, whom I'd avoided eye contact with, tapped me on the shoulder. I had to will my body to unfreeze. The synth god had initiated physical contact with me.

"What's wrong?" Synth God asked.

It was much harder to channel Christiane's casual manner talking to Alan than it had been with Martin, but I somehow managed to summon what I'd learned of method acting during sophomore year to assume a cool yet aloof attitude. "I've been trying to get a drink forever," I said, paying careful attention not to let my voice rise into a Long Island whine, "and no matter what I do, she won't look at me." I nearly choked when I realized the unintentional double-entendres I'd spewed.

Alan laughed, a full-throated hearty laugh that was as worthy of recording as any of his songs. "You've got to assert yourself. Be aggressive. Go after what you want." He couldn't possibly have understood the irony of those words.

"But I've tried, I can't," I insisted.

He locked eyes and put a reassuring hand on my shoulder. If I could have stayed in that position for twenty years, it wouldn't have been long enough. "Sure you can. I know you can." He raised his glass in salute to my quest and, having received his orders, I had no choice but to return to the bar. This time, I got my beverage. And I can say with certainty it tasted far better than any I'd ever had before.

Throughout the evening, I spotted Fletch mingling with everyone he ran into—roadies, Marxmen, fans, even waitstaff. Alan continued his conversation with Tommy and Andy Franks. Martin bopped his curly blond head with such persistent energy that I began to think he had a chemical imbalance that refused to let him remain still. Dave, however, remained his ever-elusive self.

I sat on a stool at the railing next to Marta and we sorted out the mess from earlier. She wasn't angry, she admitted, just saddened that it was me and not her who had made connections and was being invited into private rooms. I didn't point out the irony that it was she who had promised we would meet the band, as I'm sure this fact had as much to do with her depression as it being our final night of partying on the Depeche circuit.

Out of the corner of my eye, I saw Alan approach the railing and stand inches away, his leather-clad bottom practically touching my hand. I glanced over at Marta, who was so overcome by my expression that she was forced to turn away as hysterics racked her body. I thought of Alan's advice from only a little while earlier but couldn't bring myself to start a conversation, too worried that the wrong words would pour out and I'd make an even bigger gaffe than drooling on his thigh.

I became a little more courageous later on when Martin chose to slouch against the wall near me. Before I'd left on my trip, I'd made a list of questions to ask the band, the tried-and-true-fan list of lyrics, symbolism, and influences that had kept me awake into the small hours of the night as I listened to their CDs on repeat. I had a spiral notebook overflowing with lyrics of every song they'd ever recorded, as well as songs from bootlegs. No fewer than five albums of magazine and newspaper clippings sat on my bookcase next to the tour pins, concert programs, and unauthorized biographies that I'd bought on my Chinese takeout wages. The more information I accumulated, the more questions that arose, and I'd made it a point to memorize the most important ones on the off chance I'd have the opportunity to ask one of them in person.

I don't think Martin realized he was only inches from my face when he exhaled a cloud of vapors, but I still managed to ask him the meaning of "Pimpf," a song from *Music for the Masses*.

Still singing his own tune, Martin answered in one long but surprisingly coherent run-on sentence. "It's the name of the group of youngest Nazi children, not that I'm condoning it or anything, just that they all jumped right into it without thinking about it and that's what I did with this song." Once again he smiled and nodded, and had dismissed me with those two simple gestures. After thanking him, I watched as he stood, wobbled over to the bar, and ordered another drink. It was then that I realized, before I'd left New York, that his one mundane answer was more than I'd ever hoped to achieve on this journey, that the multiple interactions with my idols were beyond what I could ever have comprehended when my father plunked down his Amex for my plane ticket. That one answer alone, I thought as I walked back to the bar, was worth the credit card interest.

Marta had found Dave. He was dancing with "The Bitch," an Italian girl who had managed to flirt her way into each of the guys' arms at one stop or another during their Iberian tour. She had a body that rocked but her face wasn't quite up to what Marta thought was befitting of her beloved. My companion shook her head as the lead singer claimed the dance floor for himself, his bodyguards circling him and The Bitch so that no one could pass. Several club patrons, unaware of Dave's fame, looked on in disgust as they were corralled into a space far too small for so many people. "Who does he think he is?" Marta asked, her opinion of the lead singer having completely reversed now that he'd chosen someone else's dance card. "Why is he so important that he can push all those others off the floor?" Her upper lip curled as The Bitch began a slow, grinding dance against Dave. It was almost too much for Marta to take.

"We should call her The Slut, not The Bitch," she declared. She then related how she had seen the long-legged Italian tramp lead Martin up to the fourth floor only an hour earlier. When the songwriter descended the stairs a while later, his hair was mussed and his face bright red. In a separate incident, she'd seen Martin make a mad dash for the bathroom, which she presumed was to vomit, before sauntering out straight back to the bar. "He was only making room for more," she explained.

As per our custom, we left the dance club after the sun had risen. The morning light was a harsh reality, but every party must end. It was a pill we always swallowed with reluctance.

10

There is no harsher reality than a bus station after a night of partying with your idols. The long bus ride looming ahead of us—from Barcelona to Madrid, then north to León—only dampened our already trampled spirits.

Our adventure had taken its toll on Marta. In a rare display of weakness, she admitted regret at having attended the concerts, citing her disappointment with the behavior of her idols and the fact she now had a heightened—if that were possible—obsession with the band. Although I didn't quite follow her line of reasoning, I listened as she confessed irritation with her own behavior. "This journey has changed me, Jenn." She couldn't bring herself to look me in the eye. "And I'm not sure I like all of the changes." I waited for further explanation, but either she was too tired or too embarrassed to elaborate.

We managed to sleep most of the way to the capital city and were blessed with a half-empty bus that allowed us each to sprawl across a row of seats. When we arrived at our destination in the early afternoon, we learned that the bus for the next leg of our journey wouldn't leave for several hours, which meant we'd be passing the time replenishing our ebbing strength at the closest cafetería. Although the thought of yet another bocadillo was anything but appealing, the conflict between my vegetarianism and the Spanish cuisine left little option.

As we waited out our departure, I used the time to finish a few postcards and jot notes in my journal. Although Marta had initially ridiculed my compulsion to write as frequently as possible, she was now thankful for my habit and asked me to read some of my entries so that we could relive the events. I indulged her for a while but stopped when she became upset at my verbal editing, suspicious that I'd written unflattering comments about her. Her innuendos and the still-present nagging itch made me decide it was finally time for a call home.

Before leaving, my mother had agreed that I need call only once a week at most, the trans-Atlantic phone rate being too pricey for anything more frequent. It was now almost one week since my departure, and as I rummaged through my purse to find enough pesetas to make the call, I rehearsed how I would relate my tale, in as brief a manner as possible. I'd of course have to edit out the fact that we had left León without the knowledge of Marta's parents, but I figured the call would be short enough that I could do most of the talking. What few questions my mother could squeeze in could easily be dodged. I began practicing my abbreviated tale and for a moment the nagging itch was replaced with a rush of adrenaline as I relived the excitement of traveling in a new country and fulfilling my dream of meeting the band. I was as euphoric about the memories as I was at the thought of being able to flaunt them to my mother, whose negative words still rung in my hand like post-concert tinnitus.

I left Marta with our bags and found a pay phone off in a corner where the din of the terminal would be least bothersome. The pesetas clinked through the device and soon enough the pleasant tone of an American ring was heard on the other end. But when I heard the voice on the other line, that nagging itch began clawing at my insides. It was my aunt, and although it was not wholly unusual for her to visit my home, her customary over-effusiveness was replaced with a somber tone. When she heard my voice, she said nothing before passing the phone to my mother.

"I met them, Mom. I met Depeche Mode," I began babbling, happy to be able to prove her wrong in her assessment of my trip. "I went backstage, I got their autographs, I even spoke with them—"

"Where are you?" my mom asked, her voice almost unrecognizable in its unsteady pitch that cut me short. The itch turned into a chill that froze every muscle of my body.

"Spain, I'm still here. I don't go to France for a few days, remember?" My voice was tentative. Something was definitely wrong.

I heard her inhale deeply, which took longer than her frugal manner should have dictated while on an international line. "Well, I have some good news and some bad news."

"I know, Roberta had her baby," I finished for her, relaying the news about my new cousin, which I'd learned from a call with my sister a few days earlier.

"Yes, and he's fine." She paused and I heard her heave a great sigh from the other side of the ocean. "But your father had a heart attack and... He's gone, hon. I want you to come home."

* * *

Marta found me lying crumpled in a squalid corner of the bus station, the receiver still firmly grasped in my hand. It took her a few moments to decipher my mangled words and discern what had caused my breakdown. When realization hit, her face paled, but she managed to maintain her composure, absorbing me in her arms even as my sobbing intensified. We sat huddled together for an indeterminate time, my tears finally abating until I was collected enough to stand.

I allowed myself to be led back to the bench, where our belongings still lay untouched, and wiped my eyes as I sat down. The full impact had yet to hit me, and I picked up my journal to continue where I'd left off. Marta placed a gentle hand on the blank page before me.

"Do you think you should?"

I nodded, unable to glance at her face, which I knew would contain emotions I was not yet willing to acknowledge. "I'm not going to write about this. I'm just going to finish the entry I started." My hand shook as I put pen to paper, but I was determined to write, if only to busy myself with such inconsequential matters as rock stars and nightclubs.

The ink spilled onto the pages, my mind focused on relating the events of the past few days down to the very last detail. I became so absorbed in the task that I didn't notice that Marta had left my side until she returned.

"Sabina is coming," she told me. I didn't understand what this meant and continued scribbling without looking up. "She's going to take us to the airport."

Again I nodded, not yet strong enough to engage in verbal communication about this latest turn of events. I was still writing when Sabina arrived to lead us to the car.

I sat behind the driver, someone whose name I've since forgotten, probably a relative of Sabina's. The late-afternoon heat made air conditioning a necessity, but I needed something real, something not produced by motors or engines or electronic gadgetry, and so rolled down the window to the hot gust of air that slapped me in the face. For the entire ride to the airport, I kept my head aimed into the arid breeze that assailed my eyes, so that when I finally went to open them, the salt of my tears had nearly glued them shut.

Once at the airport, I rang my mother again and explained that I'd run out of money during my previous call. The only flights that would bring me home in time for the funeral were well over a thousand dollars, and although I still had more than enough left in the wad of petty cash my father had given me, my mother and I agreed that I shouldn't take the flight, that the chances of my making it in time, due to the time difference, were slim. I later learned that the funeral, which according to Jewish law should have taken place within twenty-four hours of my father's passing, had already been delayed beyond the mandated limit. After a tearful discussion, my mother and I agreed that I would stay on in Europe as originally planned, that I would leave for France a few days ahead of schedule. I later realized this was so my mother could be assured I'd now be in safe hands.

I phoned Marion and informed her of my change in plans, my head failing to switch languages so that I ended up speaking in a Spanish-French patois that only succeeded in confusing her. But after several attempts, my words became clear, and I heard her break down as she realized my father, with whom she'd spent the previous summer, had passed. She wished me *gros bisous* and told me she'd see me in a few days, that her entire family was looking forward to meeting me. Still in a daze, I hung up the phone and avoided Marta's glance. I couldn't manage to look her square in the face.

It was as if I had been shut off from the rest of the world by a transparent box that warped all outside sights and sounds. I was aware of people speaking around me but not the words, which rose and fell as if they came from next-door neighbors in a badly insulated apartment. The nagging itch was gone, replaced by a numbness that hijacked my senses. At Marta's guidance, I moved from one location to the next, hardly aware of my surroundings at any given moment.

Sabina's family invited us to spend the night, since we'd missed the last bus to León. Her mother apologized for the accommodations, as her home was undergoing extensive remodeling, but I wouldn't have noticed if there'd been a backhoe in the living room. At ten o'clock, with the belated Spanish sun just beginning to set, we sat down in the yard for the evening meal. I fished pieces of tuna from the pasta salad, hoping not to offend, but given the circumstances, I probably would have been forgiven even if I'd begun to fling food like a two-year-old.

When I asked if it would be okay to take a shower, I was forewarned of the lack of hot water, but I didn't care. The icy liquid seemed a lenient penitence after the offenses I'd committed. When Sabina's mother burst into the bathroom to bring me a towel, I barely so much as flinched, despite my reticence at being seen completely naked. Not long after, I gave myself over to sleep. My dreams were almost worse than my reality.

I sit around my dinette table with John, Dimitria, and my cousin Brietta, all of us nattering on about trivial matters—SATs, college applications, end-of-summer parties. Only Britt and I know of my father's passing, and we keep the knowledge to ourselves. It's late at night, the same time my father often returned from his business at the bar, and we hear the familiar patter of footsteps thudding down

216

the stairs, the floorboards squeaking in a rhythm distinct to him. I freeze. Brietta and I look at each other, each equally frightened. Then we hear my father's distinctive cough. "What's wrong?" Dimitria asks. "It's only your *father*."

The footsteps grow louder until the house is almost shaking. "But my father is dead," I tell her. On cue, my father enters the kitchen, bloated, sallow, and completely unaware that he is no longer alive.

* * *

We caught a three o'clock bus, which included a stopover in what I assumed was the same location where we had rested on my initial journey to Marta's town. Our bus pulled into León in late afternoon and we walked in silence to Marta's home from the station. As we stood across the street from her front door, a car pulled into the driveway. "My father has arrived," she said without emotion. The phrase carried more weight than was intended.

We sat in her living room, her parents, Estevo, and I trying to understand each other as much as the language barrier would allow. One of Señor Paredes's first questions—which I understood all too well—was if I knew about my father's passing, and he asked Estevo to translate, not trusting his own daughter. Yes, I knew about his death, I answered, and, yes, I knew about the Iberian flight that might have brought me to the funeral on time. For the time being, that was all they had for me.

Then Marta got hers. I didn't understand most of the words that flew past me, but I could tell that her parents had put out a missing person's report—something that would remain on Marta's record the rest of her life—and that they had believed me to be a minor. Until that moment, neither Marta nor I had understood how far our obsession had taken us. We could now visualize the storm that had been raining down while we were out dancing under strobe lights and consuming far too many fruity beverages with rock stars.

After our sermon, we were dismissed, and Marta led me up to her bedroom. When she saw that all of the Depeche Mode memorabilia had been removed, she broke down in tears. The collection that she had exalted since our very first correspondence was nowhere to be seen, her parents having removed every last artifact. Fragments of tape and empty spaces on her bookshelves were all that remained.

Although we'd been awake only a few hours, I felt the need to sleep, and Marta made up my bed so that I could fall into another nightmare-ridden slumber.

This time, when my father enters the kitchen with his yellow face and bloated body, I inform him that he is dead. My friends gape in horror as he nods, the movement causing his rotted head and then each of his limbs to fall off and lie in a decaying pile on the yellow linoleum.

* * *

Over the next two days, I slept an inordinate amount of time, waking in the late morning even after having gone to sleep in the early hours of evening. Cynthia, who was staying at casa Paredes, occasionally checked in on my progress, poking a curious head into the room of the sleeping American. Julio also stopped by, first to drop off the Suitcase From Hell and later to inquire on my well-being. Surprised at my recently acquired ability to speak basic Spanish, he took it upon himself to apologize once again for his poor interpretation of the Springsteen song. I felt sorry for his luck when he unwittingly blasted the radio to hear his new favorite song, "Tears in Heaven," only to see him redden when Marta informed him of the meaning of the lyrics.

One night, while watching Marta and Cynthia give a performance of traditional Spanish dances, I received a call from Ilene. I learned that she and my brother-in-law would be in Hamburg on business just days later, and she asked if I would like to join them. As I watched my Spanish friends slap their heels and clack imaginary castanets, my only thoughts were of home and family, and home meant only wherever my family currently was—whether that be Manhattan, Long Island, or Hamburg.

"I'll see you soon," I told Ilene, and hung up the phone, watching two strangers dance rhythms choreographed ages ago. Marta's face fell when I told her I'd be leaving in just a few hours.

* * *

The train whistle had already sounded when Marta placed the Suitcase From Hell in my compartment. She threw it in the corner with gusto, wiping her hands of whatever illness it might have borne.

Since returning to León, we hadn't spoken of our adventures on the road, not even to Cynthia, whose curiosity was tempered only by the delicacy of my situation. Once or twice, while in the middle of some mundane activity such as a meal or watching a Spanish-dubbed version of *Dirty Dancing*, Marta and I would exchange glances. Sometimes they were elative, sometimes remorseful, sometimes our eyes communicated the many conflicting emotions that we'd experienced during our first week of friendship. But always, and I'm not quite sure how, we seemed to be feeling the very same emotion at the very same moment.

Without discussing it, I knew that neither of us was yet sure whether or not we regretted our decisions of the past week, and we couldn't admit that to anyone but each other. We knew what pain we had caused ourselves and many, many others, but we were still riding the wake of euphoria that had persisted despite the tragic denouement. Few could understand what had driven us to do what we had done, and even fewer could comprehend why we felt as we did just then. Such was the bond that had joined us before we'd even exchanged that very first letter.

After relieving herself of the Suitcase From Hell for the last time, Marta turned to me and, even as the train heaved beneath us, took me tightly in her arms, unwilling to part. "I'm not the same person," she reminded me. "Our adventure changed me. You changed me."

I refused to let go, partly due to my unwillingness to show emotion. But what had I learned during my European excursion if not to let loose my feelings?

"Go, get off, or you'll find yourself in Hamburg in no short time." I pushed her away, averting my head to hide reddening eyes.

I heard the compartment door swoosh open and turned to see Marta standing in the threshold. "I'm not the same," she repeated, then turned and walked down the aisle, the train picking up speed even as I chased her.

She stepped off onto the platform, Julio and Cynthia flanking her in support. Well after their silhouettes had disappeared, I remained on the staircase waving into the blackness that filled the world behind the train.

ABOUT THE AUTHOR

Jenna Rose Robbins is a writer and editor who has ghostwritten more than 12 books, including two *New York Times* bestsellers. After graduating from the University of Michigan, Jenna went on to receive her Master's of Professional Writing from the University of Southern California. When she's not getting eyestrain at her computer, Jenna can generally be found trying to avoid emergency rooms around the world.

www.jennarobbins.com